The Struggle for a Happy Ending:
Book one – Trapped Heart

First Edition

ISBN: 978-1-7395841-0-8

The Struggle for a Happy Ending:

Book one

Trapped Heart

I'm Loren, I am a mother of three, a student, an aspiring entrepreneur, and the author of Trapped Heart. This is my first romance story, and I am very pleased to share it with you. This book will be a trilogy, book two and three to follow. I love writing and have enjoyed it ever since I was a little girl and I hope to continue to share my passion with my readers.

TRAPPED HEART

Loren Aviva Haigh

Chapter 1

Cindy lay in the bed still as a rock, waiting for the guy to fall asleep. She knew it wouldn't be long now, they always drifted off within minutes, seconds even of their passion being spent. True enough, the man's breathing deepened and turned to snores. One hand was still draped across her top half, his pink skin against her brown, under the t-shirt she hadn't bothered taking off. She rolled slightly to the side and it slipped out, its dead weight flopping onto the bed. The man snored louder and rolled away from her, deep in his post-coital slumber.

That was her cue. She slung her legs over the side of the dirty mattress and fished her knickers and mini skirt from the floor where they had been discarded. She dressed quickly, pulled her thick curls into a bun and grabbed the crumpled notes left on the bed-stand next to the dimly lit alarm clock. 4.10am. She counted the money, picked up her heels and jacket and tiptoed out of the room.

The rest of the house was littered with evidence of the party. Bodies asleep everywhere, empty cans, bottles and tell-tale streaks of white powder on the coffee tables. In the kitchen she found a half packet of Custard Creams and a can of Coke which she threw in her handbag. No one stirred as she stepped over sleeping bodies in the hallway and let herself out the front door and into the icy November dawn.

She sat on the front step to buckle on her heels and wrapped her fake-fur jacket around her. It did little to keep the cold away and her bare legs shivered and prickled as she walked down the empty street. Her heels click-clacked loudly on the pavement, the only sound to be heard as the city slowly awoke.

Cindy wandered if the Tube was running yet. It would be warmer than waiting at the freezing bus stop and she'd be home in ten minutes, enough time to get some sleep before Callum had to get up for school. But she dismissed the thought – she couldn't afford to spend her cut of the night's takings on tube fare. Her bus pass would have to do, as always, and she'd just have to endure the hour and a half it took the night bus to get there... She would just be there in time to make Callum his breakfast, walk him to school and then she could grab a couple of hours' sleep.

Her feet were numb from the cold and tight straps by the time she got to the bus stop. A man in his forties was perched on the thin bench, smoking.

Cindy offered him a wan smile as they exchange glances, the man's eyes lingering on her body and her long, chocolate brown legs. She self-consciously tugged her skirt down a little, even though it didn't budge an inch.

"Long night?" The man smirked, his eyes suggesting that he knew exactly what Cindy had been up to.

"Party." she offered and pulled her jacket tighter around her. She brought her thighs close together and turned her body slightly away from him, pretending to study the timetable.

"Young thing like you shouldn't be wandering around alone" the man took a drag of his cigarette, now studying the view from the back that she had unintentionally offered him. Cindy turned around and pushed herself into the corner of the shelter, holding her tiny handbag in front of her legs, covering what little she could.

"You know, bus stops are non-smoking areas" she spat at him. The man shrugged, took a last drag and put the cigarette out under his foot. Mercifully, the lights from the bus swept around the corner and he didn't bother Cindy anymore.

The bus pulled up and the man stepped aside with a chivalrous gesture for Cindy to get on first. She mumbled a thanks and climbed on, hurrying up the steps to the top deck, knowing full well that his eyes were up her skirt as she did so. Thankfully he stayed on the bottom level and she flopped in her customary seat at the front. The bus jerked forward and soon she was lulled into a doze under the harsh lights and stale hot air of the heated interior.

***

It was past 6am when Cindy dragged herself up the stairs of the council block to the small flat on the 6th floor. The lift was still out of order from when the squatters in number 56 smashed the control panel and Cindy's climb home had become a Golgotha of endless stairs, peppered with chewing gum and smelling of piss in the corners. She just let her mind go blank and placed one foot slowly in front of the other until eventually she was standing outside her front door.

Well, not her front door exactly but still, a home of sorts. She was lucky to have it and lucky for Jim who had taken them in when she had nowhere else to go. She slid the key into the lock and quietly, carefully let herself in, trying not to wake anyone.

"You're late." Jim's voice came from the kitchenette. Cindy kicked off the painful heels and huddled over the small radiator that was just coming on by the door. Jim's bulky frame appeared in the hallway behind her. He was in his boxers, his dark, muscular torso exposed as he didn't feel the cold. "I take it it was a good night?" In his hand was a hot cup of tea and his six-pack rippled as he brought it up to his lips. Cindy never tired of how fit he was.

"Just the one." Cindy said and not moving from the radiator she fished out the money from her bag and handed it to him. Jim handed her the tea and counted it with a frown.

"You can do better than one a night babe" he pulled a fiver out of the cash and handed it to her. "The more you make the more you get to keep, right?" He kissed her on the lips and pocketed the rest. "God you're frozen! Drink that tea, I'll make another." "Thanks babe" Cindy gratefully clutched the hot mug in her hands and sipped. "Is Callum up?"

"Not yet." Jim disappeared back into the kitchenette and she heard him flick the kettle switch. "Go have a shower, warm you up. I'm going to
Clapham so I'll see you tonight."

"Ok." Cindy took her tea and padded barefoot down the narrow hallway to the box room at the end. It was still too early to wake Callum but she opened the door quietly and snuck in. Her five year old son lay fast asleep in a tangled heap of covers and teddies. She loved looking at his face, so angelic and peaceful as he slept, before he would wake and turn into the boisterous little boy that stopped for no one during the day. She leaned in and planted a kiss on his soft head. His curls fell loose around his head like a halo, not tight like hers and lighter in colour. His skin was still babysoft and light brown like milk in coffee. He stirred but didn't wake. Let him sleep, she thought and tidied the covers around him. Let him stay in his dreamland as long as possible, before dragging him back to his sad reality of handed-down school shoes and charity shop uniform.

Cindy watched him breathe gently, his little chest rise and fall, his fingers long but still pudgy with toddler-fat. He was starting to change, to grow into a young boy but she could still see remnants of her baby around the edges. He adored Jim and although she had explained to him that he was not his real daddy, he was as much a father to him as anyone would be. And Cindy didn't mind. Callum's real father was a blur from her raging teen years. In fact, he could be any of the boys she had partied with during that Christmas of
2014…

At 16 years old Cindy had already been living rough for two years. The streets had been bad but the hostels and care homes had been worse, with noisy roommates and often staff who cared more for what was between her legs than her actual welfare. No, Cindy was a survivor and hadn't left her own shitty parents to end up being pushed around by some stranger instead. She found people who really cared for her, people just like her who became her friends and sometimes boyfriends. She gave them what they wanted and got what she wanted in return – a warm place to stay, food to eat and the occasional treat. Alcohol, weed, coke or pills, she wasn't picky. Anything that took her away from her fucked-up reality was welcome.

Callum let out a little snore and turned over. He was still fast asleep, so Cindy crept out of his room and into the bathroom. She had time for a quick shower. The bathroom was still freezing so she ran the hot water and stripped off her clothes standing by the radiator. Soon steam began to fill the tiny space and her skin stopped prickling. She tested the water, adjusted the temperature and stepped under the hot stream with relief. Everything melted away, the fatigue, the painful cold and the grunts of the party-boy from that night. She lathered her flannel and wiped herself clean. Naked, her skin now showed the signs of the night – she noticed a small bruise on her hip and another around her arm where his hands had squeezed her. She swore under her breath. Asshole. Bruises were a right put-off plus she had to hide them well or nosy mums in the schoolyard started asking questions. She didn't give a shit about what they thought of her, but there was Callum to think about. If their stupid gossiping got to the Head, it was only one phone call away from social services knocking on their door. And she'd been down that route once before.

Of course, social services had been on her case the moment she had turned up at the walk-in clinic, pregnant at 16 and with no parents in tow. She had managed to fob them off by convincing her boyfriend at the time to claim he was the father and they stayed at bay until the baby was born. Of course, then they started hounding her a bit more but she was smart. She turned up to all the baby clinics, the check-ups and Callum's vaccinations were all up to date. She didn't give them a single reason to doubt her ability to care for her son and despite their efforts, she held on to him tooth and nail. He was her everything.

However, the boyfriend had zero interest in being a family man. In all fairness he hadn't put them on the street but he made it clear that Cindy needed to find a new arrangement. They hadn't been together for months anyway and he was already seeing other girls, which was fine by her. She was ready to move on as always. And that was where Jim came in.

She had known him for a while, as he did business with her boyfriend and was around the flat often. He'd always been friendly and Cindy could tell he was also interested in her but had kept his distance out of respect. She liked that in a man, respect. He treated her politely and always asked if she and the baby needed anything. Whenever he came around there would always be something for Callum, a pack of nappies, baby food, money (he would jokingly say it was for sweets although they both knew it was for her).

Over time she was charmed. Here was a man who treated her and her child with kindness, and who wasn't entirely bad looking either. So Cindy swooped in and made it known, indirectly, that she was single again and needed to move out. Temporarily of course, just until she got a job and found her feet, then the council would home her and the child. Jim had offered his place instantly and within months they had become a family of sorts.

The bathroom door opened and Jim's head stuck in.

"I'm heading off, beautiful."

“Ok. See you later” Cindy wiped the steam off the glass and waved at him sleepily. Jim blew her a kiss and shut the door behind him.

Yes, she was lucky indeed to have a home, she thought, watching the glass steam up again. She fingered the bruise on her arm. A home, a beautiful son and a loving man.

So why did she feel so empty?

***

Chapter 2

"Callum! No!" Cindy yanked Callum's hand just as he leapt for the puddle, pulling him away from the muddy water. "Stop it, you'll get soaked!" she held him close under her large umbrella and hurried him over the pedestrian crossing. The rain started to pour in earnest.

"Mummy, slow down!" Callum whined, planting his feet. Cindy sighed and awkwardly, holding the umbrella with one hand, picked him up.

"I'm sorry baby. I just don't want you to be late." She planted a kiss on his cheek and he held on to her neck as she trotted down the pavement to the school gates. Parents were already walking out, leaving after dropping off their children.

"Better late than never!" joked one of the dads as she ran past. She didn't turn to reply but bee-lined for the entrance and the safety of the dry building. It was always a pain rushing to school in the rain but she was grateful for the excuse to cover up in the weather – the scarf around her neck was perfectly hiding the love-bite she had also discovered after her shower…

She put Callum down on his feet and folded the brolly, leaving it against the wall with the selection of other dripping brollies. She then adjusted her scarf and walked Callum to reception.

"So sorry we're late." She said to Mrs Evans, the receptionist. "We couldn't find his wellies."

"Oh, not to worry." Mrs Evans beamed. "You got to have your wellies on a day like this, right Callum?" Callum smiled at the friendly woman. "Besides, you're not the only one."

Cindy turned to see a mum about her age and a young boy rush in, almost soaked to the bone.

"Logan!" Callum exclaimed and waved. The boy waved in return and his mother rushed him to Mrs Evans.

"So sorry…" she began but Mrs Evans raised a hand, interrupting her.

"Not to worry. Lots of people have been delayed this morning. Ok, boys, say bye bye to your mummies and I'll take you to your classroom." Cho continued in a pleasant but business-like tone. Callum and Logan dutifully gave their mothers a kiss each, took their bags and followed Mrs Evans down the corridor.

"It only rains at drop-off and pick-up, doesn't it?" the woman smiled at Cindy, wringing her blonde hair out on the carpeted floor. Cindy smiled back.

"Yeah, what's with that, right?" They walked together towards their discarded umbrellas, peering at the state of the weather outside.

"I might wait till it holds off a bit…" Cindy mused, watching the rain hammer down.

"Yeah, good idea. So, you're Callum's mum?"

"Yes."

"I'm Becky. Logan's mum." She held a hand out and Cindy shook it politely. "He doesn't shut up about Callum. Apparently they're joined at the hip those two."

"Really? I didn't know that."

"Oh yeah, thick as thieves apparently."

Cindy smiled. Callum had only started at that school a few weeks ago and it was good to hear he was making friends. She suddenly realised she hadn't introduced herself.

"Oh, sorry. I'm Cindy."

"Nice to meet you. Do you live nearby?"

"Yeah, abut ten minutes' walk."

"Twenty in this weather and a small child in tow…" Becky retorted and they laughed. Cindy wasn't usually bothered about mingling with the other parents but she found she liked Becky. And they were the same age, unlike most other parents who seemed older and judgmental.

The rain began to ease off and Cindy yawned at the thought of getting home to a few hours' kip in her warm bed.

"Looks like you need a coffee." Becky said. "That café round the corner is nice, if you fancy one."

"Oh, that sounds lovely, but it's sleep I need, not coffee…" Cindy smiled and added "I… work nights."

"Oh. Ok." Becky looked disappointed.

"But another time, I'd love to. We could get the boys together too, for a playdate?"

"Yeah that sounds nice. Why don't you come to mine? I'm free on Thursdays."

"Sure, Thursday is good."

"What's your number?" Becky pulled out her phone and typed in the number Cindy gave her. She then hit "dial" and Cindy's phone rang deep in her coat pocket. She pulled it out and saved the number.

"There we go. Now we have each other's numbers." Becky smiled. "I'll text you my address."

"Cool. Thanks. I'll bring cake."

"Oooh, sounds like a deal! I better get to work, looks like there's a clear patch now."

They smiled at each other and ducked out of the door, hurrying through the playground.

"Hope you catch some Z's!" Becky waved at Cindy at the gates as they went off in separate directions.

"Thanks! See you Thursday!" Cindy called back at her. Then, with grin on her face, trotted the ten minutes back to the flat and her cosy duvet.

***

It was lunchtime when Jim nuzzled her neck, softly nibbling her skin, waking her up gently.

"Mmm..." she murmured, turning over slightly disorientated. "What time...?"

"It's nearly one o'clock." Jim slid under the covers with her, his cool body pressing against her bed-warm skin. His hand slid down her waist, stroking her tummy. "You don't want to sleep all day; you won't be able to go to bed tonight." His hand travelled further down.

"So, this is how you wake me up?" Cindy turned but let him kiss her lips.

"Is it working?" Jim whispered as his hand moved under her knickers. Cindy moaned softly and as her hands went to his waist, she realised he was already naked. They kissed and Jim's large hands slid her knickers down as he positioned himself above her. She parted her legs and let him slide inside her, buckling to his rhythm, moaning louder and louder as his thrusting became more and more insistent.

Within seconds, he was spent. It was never really "lovemaking" with Jim, but Cindy enjoyed pleasing him, it made her feel like she had something to give in return for all he provided for her and Callum. And it made her feel good too, if not satisfied. She had seen how other girls looked at him, his bulging muscles and handsome, manly face. But they didn't have him, he was hers and that gave her something to be smug about when their jealous eyes fell on her.

She caressed his back as he lay on top of her, panting, catching his breath. His lips stroked her ear and kissed it. "God babe I needed that" he whispered "you're so damn hot" he kissed and nibbled and rolled off her, lying beside her. She nestled her still-sleepy head on his chest and felt it rise and fall with each breath.

"No wonder you're so in demand" He kissed the top of her head and ran his fingers lightly along her spine, tickling her. "I gotta be careful none of them boys steal you off me."

"They're just customers, babe, you know that." She purred, lifting her face to look at him. "Don't mean nothing."

"That's what I like to hear." His eyes locked on hers and his hand came up to her nipple, playing with it, tugging and squeezing. She laughed, and he tugged a little harder.

"I don't have to worry about any of them, do I?" he squeezed a bit more and she yelped.

"Of course not. Jim, come on!"

He let go and raised himself on an elbow, bringing his mouth down to her breast. He put his lips around her sore nipple, sucked it gently and kissed it.

"Right answer." He said and got up. "Sorry, you know I get jealous babe."

"It's ok." Cindy whispered and got out of bed. Jim pulled on his trousers and headed to the kitchen.

"I'll make us some sandwiches. Coffee?"

"Yes please. Thanks" Cindy padded naked to the bathroom and turned the shower on for the second time that day. Jim went to the kitchen and she stepped under the water stream.

Twenty minutes later, she was sitting at the small kitchen table, wolfing down lunch with Jim. It had been hours since that morning's cup of tea and the single slice of toast she had managed to eat while getting Callum ready for school. After dropping him off, the night's fatigue had finally caught up with her and she'd gone straight to bed without breakfast.

Jim poured more coffee in their cups. "Gary called while you were in the shower. There's a party tonight at his mate's place. I'm gonna pop down with some treats for them."

Jim's "treats" was the other half of their income. Cindy had known them all well in her younger years but had promptly stopped when she fell pregnant. And since Callum came along it was only the occasional smoke or popper she indulged in. Jim also made sure of that. He said he wanted her to always be clearheaded when taking in clients, so many girls got in trouble of passed out and let clients get away without paying too. Plus, he didn't want his babe getting hooked on any crap. Cindy was grateful that he looked out for her that way. Sure, she didn't exactly love her "job" but Jim made sure she was safe and that was the most important thing.

"Do you want me to come?" She offered. She would have to find someone to look after Callum for the night.

"Yeah, I think it'll be a good crowd. Gary knows people with good money, we can make a killing tonight. I already asked Milly next door if she can watch Callum for a couple of hours."

He thought of everything. Cindy smiled. Milly was the next-door neighbour's daughter. She was 16, reliable and Cindy liked her. She often babysat for them and Cindy didn't mind the expense – Milly reminded her of herself at 16 and it was nice to know that she was helping her earning some honest money instead of roaming the streets and stealing to survive like she had done at her age.

"OK, sounds good."

"What have you got to wear?" Jim asked. Cindy thought of what was left in her wardrobe – she'd not been to the launderette yet this week and most of her party clothes were in the wash bin in the bathroom.

"I've got the leather mini skirt…"

"Not the trashy looking stuff, I think these guys like classier girls." Jim interrupted. "Don't you have like a cocktail dress or anything?"

"Not really." The sort of parties Jim sent her to where mostly students and ravers, a short skirt and crop top were more than appropriate for those types of gatherings. "I can smarten the skirt up a bit. I have a glitter blouse and accessories; I'll figure it out."

"Ok, do that. I guess you should go shopping this week too" he pulled his wallet out and counted a few notes that he handed to her "get you some nicer stuff yeah?"

Cindy beamed. "Cheers babe. Yeah, I'll find some nice dresses."

Jim stood up, scraping his chair on the kitchen lino. He picked up their plates and put them in the sink. “Oh, and wear those fuck-me boots, you know the ones.”

“The knee-length ones?”

“Yeah, they’re hot. They’ll turn some heads alright.” He smiled at her and she felt her cheeks flush.

He was always complimenting her. She stood up.

“I’m gonna get ready to fetch Callum. I’ve gotta go to the shop too.” She went over and kissed him on the cheek as he washed up the dishes. He turned to her as she walked out the kitchen.

“Oh, and babe?”

“Yeah?”

“Don’t waste the night on just one client, yeah? Plenty of fish, ok?”

“Sure thing babe.” She smiled and nodded but inside her chest, her heart beat a little faster. *Just a job*, she reminded herself. *Just a job and nothing more*.

***

Chapter 3

The guy Jim had picked for her was 25, decked in designer gear from head to toe and coked up to his eyeballs. He pressed her against the cold tiles of the bathroom and thrust harder, faster.

"Slow down darling" Cindy grunted, but he wasn't listening, already caught in the throes of his climax. He jerked once, twice and collapsed against her, sandwiching her between himself and the wall.

"Fuck me…" he muttered, dribbling a little on her shoulder, Cindy wriggled away from him just enough to feel him slip out of her. She pushed him gently, always smiling.

"That was great babe." She pulled up her knickers and pulled down her skirt, straightening herself out.

"Yeah…" the man exhaled, still catching his breath. He tucked himself away and did his trousers up. Cindy stood smiling in front of the locked door, her arms crossed. The guy sniffed loudly, his eyes wild.

"Can I go back to the party?"

“Once you’ve paid for this one first.” Cindy smiled sweetly.

“Oh, sorry.” The guy shoved his hand in his pocket and pulled out some notes. Cindy took them.

“Thank you very much. Enjoy the rest of the party.” She stepped aside and unlocked the door for him. He stumbled out without a backward glance and she shut the door again. With a sigh, she washed her face and re-applied her make up, making herself look presentable. After a few minutes she exited the bathroom and sashayed her way through the party.

Jim had set up shop in a corner of the lounge, casually standing with a drink in one hand and his coat on. Punters came up to him with cash and he produced what they wanted from one of his many hidden inside pockets. He caught sight of Cindy and winked at her. She nodded and made her way over to him, picking up a drink from the drinks table as she went past. She was parched.

“Got something for me?” Jim said as she came up to him. Cindy offered him the notes in her fist. “Nice.
Did he wear a rubber?”

"Yes, I made sure."

"Remember, it's extra if they don't want to, ok? Don't let them take the piss."

"I won't babe."

"Take a break. See that guy over there?" he looked across the room to a man around 30, chatting loudly with a group of lads.

"Yeah."

"He's next. I said you'll go over when you're ready."

"Ok." Cindy swallowed her drink but her throat remained dry. Jim patted her on the bum and turned his attention to a couple of girls coming his way.

"Ladies!" How can I be of service?" Cindy stood beside him looking pretty and interested while he conducted his business. The girls took their newly purchased pills and hurried off giggling. Jim shoved their money in his breast pocket, which was getting fuller by the minute.

"I told you this would be a good night." He grinned at Cindy. She smiled back at him. "Are you having a good time?" He tucked a loose strand of her curly hair back into her bun.

"Yeah."

"Well, when you're ready." He looked over to the waiting guy suggestively. Cindy nodded and gulped her drink. Jim winked at her and she pasted a sexy smile on her face, walking slowly over to her next customer. He spotted her coming and turned, waiting. The lads behind him started whooping and he turned sharply and shushed them. They laughed and walked away to join another conversation, leaving him and Cindy alone.

"Hi, I'm Cindy."

"Dan."

"Nice party huh?"

"Yeah, Gary throws a good one always does." Dan grinned at her. They both knew the conversation was pointless small talk. Best get it over, Cindy thought to herself.

"So, erm… wanna find a quiet spot?" Dan grinned at her like a wolf. "Got the money?"

"Right here." Dan smirked. Cindy smiled suggestively and slid her hand down his front pocket, watching his face turn from smug to the same face all men made when a hand was near their privates. She went deeper and found the tip of his penis, just under the hard roll of cash. She stroked it with a finger through the material.

"Well yeah, seems everything is in order…" she purred and expertly, slowly, withdrew her hand and walked languidly out of the room. Dan followed right behind her in a lusty trance. Cindy tried the downstairs bathroom but it was locked.

"Oh come on." Dan slid his arms around her waist and pressed himself on her buttocks, rubbing against her. "I'm not paying for bathroom sex." His hands clamped on her thighs and pulled her hips further so she felt his stiffness, firm and hard behind her. She cringed but hid her face.

"Ok babe" she said sweetly. "Let's try upstairs." She wriggled her butt suggestively on his groin and heard him groan.

"Hurry up." He panted and she took his hand, leading him up the stairs. He was already unbuckling his belt when they reached the landing and she barely had time to find an empty room before he pushed her onto her knees, bending her over the bed.

"Slowly darling..." she coaxed "don't forget the condom."

"Fuck that..." he grunted and knelt behind her, pushing up her skirt.

"Dan..." she warned him, trying to swallow her panic "you have to wear one." His hands had already pushed her knickers down.

"No I don't. He said it's ok, I'll pay more." She felt him guide himself inside her and she closed her eyes. Shit. She would have to clean herself up and that wasted time.

Just a job, she repeated her mantra as Dan's hands pushed her skirt further up her waist and grabbed her hips. He jammed himself inside her with the urgency of a madman.

"Oh, God yes, yes…" he moaned, paying no heed to Cindy's low grunts as he pounded harder, deeper. His hand travelled up her blouse and pulled at her breasts. She closed her eyes and relaxed, letting her mind go blank, remembering to moan now and then for his benefit, but she knew it was pointless. They all just got it over with as fast or as slowly as they wanted. Usually fast.

Dan's hand squeezed and pulled. His body fell on top of hers, pushing her into the mattress, his hips thrust and twisted, until he climaxed with a panting, shuddering, wolfish howl. He pushed himself deeper one last time and laughed.

"That's what I'm talking about!" He exclaimed, as if Cindy had been a mountain he had conquered. She rolled her eyes but turned to smile at him.

"Just for you baby." She said. "Glad you liked it."

Dan laughed and took the roll of money from his trousers as he pulled them up. He threw it at Cindy.

"Worth every penny."

He buckled his belt, smoothed his hair and walked out.

Cindy spent some time in the room's en-suite bathroom cleaning herself up and tidying her make up again. She locked the door and sat on the edge of the bath, taking a moment to gather her thoughts. The roll of money sat undisturbed on the cabinet where she'd left it.

She reached for it and unrolled it. Two hundred quid. Cash. She wondered who these people were who could carry around this amount of money just for "treats"...

A knock on the door made her jump.

"Cindy? You there babe?" It was Jim. Cindy rolled up the cash again and straightened her clothes out, checking herself one more time in the mirror.

"Yes. I was just getting cleaned up." She unlocked the door and greeted him with a sweet smile and the roll of cash held in front of her face for him. He grinned and took it from her like a piece of candy.

"Nice one." He winked at her. "And the night's still young."

"Sure is." Cindy tried to sound convincing and walked past him to sit on the bed. "Do you mind if I take a little break? Could use another drink."

"Yeah no worries babe. I wanted to talk to you anyway. Got something big."

"Oh? What is it?"

Jim sat next to her on the bed and took her chin in his big hand, turning her head towards him. "You're gonna love this one. So, these guys, a load of them work for like banks and stuff, in the City."

"Ok."

"Well I was talking to this guy and there's like a big do on Saturday." Cindy's heart sank a little. Jim continued "but this is like super classy, one of those big charity events or some shit posh people go to."

"Doesn't sound like the sort of thing you normally go to."

"Not me babe. You."

"What?"

"It's not for me. It'll be your own gig. Massive I'm telling you. Chandeliers and champagne and shit." "Jim, I don't understand. We always go together, you… you pick the clients."

"I've picked him already."

"What? Who?"

"Some banker Gary knows through a mate. Patrick something. See, these posh guys, they don't do these sort of parties" he pointed outside the bedroom door "they do classy affairs. You know what an escort is?"

"I think so."

"It's like a posh trick. You know, classy client, more like a date. An all-night gig." He paused for effect. "Three thousand."

"What?" Cindy's breath caught in her throat.

"Three. Thousand. Pounds." Jim said slowly. "One night."

"Oh my God. Are you sure?"

"Hey, I don't do business unless I'm sure." Cindy sat in stunned silence. She had never even dreamed of that amount of money, let alone make it in one night.

"And all I have to do is go on a date? With one guy?"

Jim nodded. "Well, you do whatever he wants of course." Cindy swallowed.

"Of course." Her mind was still reeling. Jim guffawed and slapped his hand on the bed.

"Tell you what babe, just take the rest of the night off! If this new gig works out, you can kiss these crappy parties goodbye. My girl's gonna be the classiest escort in town, I guarantee you that!" He grabbed her face and planted a kiss on her lips. "We'll be rolling in it before you know it!"

Cindy couldn't stop staring at him with surprise. His face was lit up like a Christmas tree and she suddenly couldn't help bursting out laughing. She put her hand in front of her mouth.

"I'm sorry" she snorted "it's just…"

"I know" Jim laughed with her "These rich jerks are unbelievable!"

They chuckled and he patted her knee. Cindy suddenly felt like a weight was lifted. She imagined being able to buy Callum all the new clothes he needed, all the toys he wanted. Her cut would be enormous, not the fivers and tenners she had to scrounge from what these every day punters paid them. She grinned at Jim.

"You always have the best plans baby. I'll find the perfect outfit, I'll go shopping tomorrow!"

"Spare no expense" Jim said. "Gotta spend money to make money and I know you'll look the part."

Cindy nodded and grinned back at him, already dreaming about her shopping trip the next day. She'd go to the posh shops, get something proper. Not like her usual cheap stuff from Primark. No, she'd try on all the cocktail dresses and frocks in the shops whose windows she normally looked longingly at.

Cindy grinned with delight. She was moving up

***

Chapter 4

The shop assistant knocked on the changing room door just as Cindy had stepped out of the blue dress. She pulled the door ajar just enough to stick her head out and hand the dress to the smiling girl.

"I got you the size 12 in black and the red one." She handed Cindy two identical dresses in different colours.

"Thank you so much. This one was also not right." She handed back the blue dress. "Not really my colour."

"I think think the red will look gorgeous with your skin tone" the assistant offered. Cindy took the dresses.

"I'll see what they're like, thank you." She pushed the door shut and held up the two cocktail dresses in front of her in the mirror. The black was definitely classier, but the girl was right, the red really popped against her skin.

She tried them both on. The cut was gorgeous and the size fit her like a glove. She turned this way and that in the black dress, admiring the way it clung to her curves, the low cut back revealing enough skin to look sexy but not trashy. That's why these clothes are expensive she thought. They don't only look good, they make whoever wears them look good.

Look like money. She smiled, imagining herself stepping out of a fancy car and into the posh hotel – Jim had given her all the details. She was going to be picked up in a private car and driven to the Dorchester Hotel in Mayfair. The client, Patrick, would be waiting for her there.

Mayfair! She giggled to herself, wiggling her hips in the mirror. Even though she knew she was not the same as those high-class ladies who would be there, she could pretend, just for one night that she was.

She switched to the red dress and her reflection stunned her. Still classy looking but with a real femme fatale air. She was torn. Both dresses looked perfect. She looked at the price tags - £120 each… She chewed her lip trying to make a decision and then had a thought. She got her phone out of her bag and snapped a photo of her in the mirror. Then changed back into the black dress and took another photo.

She opened her messenger app and typed a message to Jim: *Can't decide which one. What do you think?* She sent it, and the two photos and waited.

Jim's reply came in under a minute: *Woah. Sexy lady!*

Cindy smiled proudly, and typed: *Which one do you think better?*

How much? Jim's reply came. Cindy typed: *£120 each.* She waited as the little dots flashed, indicating he was typing.

Get both. Came the reply. Cindy gasped with surprise. Both? She didn't have a chance to ask as another message pinged. *Spend money to make money, remember? And they both look awesome. Don't forget accessories, get whatever you need.*

Cindy nearly burst with excitement. *Ok, will do!* She typed quickly and put her phone away. Of course she had been so engrossed in choosing a dress, she had almost forgotten about shoes, handbag, jewellery.

She had to look the part and it took more than a dress to do so.

She got changed and took the dresses to the counter. The assistant nearly fell over her trying to serve her, offering matching accessories to add to her basket. Cindy felt like Julia Roberts in Pretty Woman and relished it. She let the girl show her a range of handbags, jewellery and shoes for another half hour, frowning at this, trying on that, feeling like a queen. But she didn't let herself get too carried away. Jim said get what you need but she knew that meant within reason too. And he already paid for the two dresses.

She chose a black and a red pair of heels to match each dress and an elegant looking black clutch that would go with everything. She liked the look of the diamanté earrings, necklace and bracelet set, but thought twice about it. She went instead with a simple silver necklace and studs. Elegant, not trashy she reminded herself.

She paid the beaming assistant and marched out carrying her bags with her head high. She still had an hour before picking up Callum so she would have a look around the other shops and find somewhere to get some nice cake. It was Thursday and she and

Callum were going over to Becky's for the afternoon like they had arranged.

***

The boys skipped through the park oblivious to the calls of their mothers behind them to stay close. Becky raised her voice one more time.

"Logan Smith! If I have to call you one more time there will be NO cake!" Logan stopped in his tracks and sheepishly turned to grin at his mother, waiting.

"You too Callum, hold hands please." Callum caught up with Logan and the boys joined hands giggling, then walked calmly a few steps ahead of their mums. Becky rolled her eyes.

"I have to watch him like a hawk sometimes. Blink and he's gone!"

Cindy laughed with her. "Well, at least we've got cake to bribe them with!"

"Mummy can we play on the swings?" Logan asked and Becky shook her head.

"No darling, not today. It's too wet."

"We'll go have some hot chocolate and nice cake at your house, ok?" Cindy added as his little face melted with disappointment. He lit up and she continued "And you can show Callum your room and all your toys, yeah?"

"Yeah!" Logan shouted and pulled Callum along "Let's go!"

"Not so fast mister!" Becky, trotted up to them followed by Cindy. "Remember the road."

The boys dutifully took their mums' hands and the four made their way over the crossing to the small terraced houses at the end of the road.

Once they were inside, both boys shot up the stairs to Logan's room, stomping on the landing like a herd pf baby elephants. Cindy called up to Callum to behave himself and put her shopping bags down.

"So what have you been buying? Looks like you had a fun morning." Becky eyed up the bags.

"Oh I had to find a dress for a thing on Saturday." Cindy held up the small patisserie bag for her. “Cake?” “Yeah, let’s get the kettle on. This way” she said and Cindy followed her into the small but tidy kitchen. Becky filled the kettle and flicked it on. “Take a seat” she gestured to one of the high stools at the narrow breakfast bar and got some plates out for the cakes.

“Thank you.” Cindy said, perching on the stool. “Do you want a hand with those?”

“No it’s fine. So, tell me about this fancy do on Saturday.”

“Oh, it’s erm… just like, a date.”

Becky raised an eyebrow “Oh, lucky you, sounds nice.”

Cindy smiled and changed the subject.

“So, is it just you and Logan here?”

“Yeah. His dad lives in Scotland. He’s good though, to be fair. Kept the house payments and support.”

“Oh that’s really decent of him.”

"Yeah he's not a bad guy. Just didn't work out, you know?" The kettle pinged and she made the tea. "We were like, seventeen, partying around, didn't really plan it."

"Yeah" Cindy nodded knowingly. "Same here actually. I had Callum at sixteen. Wouldn't change him for the world though."

"Tell me about it, right?" Becky chuckled and handed Cindy a hot mug of tea. "So, are you still together?"

"Oh, what, with his dad? No."

"Oh ok, I thought the guy who picks him up sometimes..."

"That's Jim. My partner."

"Handsome fella. Becky winked at her and they giggled. Cindy found that she warmed to Becky quickly. They drank more tea, ate cake and chatted about their early day as young mums. Becky had also gone through the rigmarole of keeping social services at bay and understood Cindy's story well, without judgment. Cindy felt she could open up to her a bit more, that she was talking to an equal.

At some point the boys came rushing in demanding their share of the cake that had been promised to them. Becky served up their slices and the two women watched and listened as the boys recounted imaginary adventures to them around mouthfuls of chocolate sponge and flying crumbs.

When they returned to their games, Becky and Cindy picked up their conversation about past lives.

“I ran away at 13.” Cindy said. “I doubt my parents even noticed, to be honest.”

“I hear ya girl.” Becky nodded gravely. “If my dad wasn’t passed out drunk at home, he was either in the nick or in the pub. My mum kept kicking him out.”

“Wish mine had. She just put up with him beating on her and blamed us kids for it.”

Becky shook her head. “Some people just should be parents you know?”

"It's why I wasn't gonna let anyone take Callum away. I had to prove I wasn't like them."

Becky put her hand on Cindy's. "And you're not. You know that, right?" She smiled. Cindy smiled back. "You're so right." She turned her head towards the sound of the boys giggling in the front room. "Everything I do, it's for him. That's more that I can say about my parents."

"Amen to that sister. Same here."

Cindy sipped her tea. She had never opened up that easily to anyone before. It was wonderful to have someone who listened and understood. Becky was just like her and she knew she would like hanging out with this girl. She sensed there was a good friendship in the air.

But she wouldn't share all her secrets just yet. She would enjoy her company, but still and to test the waters about how understanding Becky might be. And the boys played so well together, it would be silly to ruin what was obviously a great friendship.

“There’s a fun fair in town next weekend.” Cindy remembered. “If the weather is dry, we could the boys? Sunday?”

“That sounds great. They’ll love it.” Becky said, then frowned “Oh, but my cousin is coming over…”

“Oh.”

“But they can come along if that’s ok? He’s got a little boy too, Tom.”

“Yeah the more the merrier. “ Cindy said “Nice for the kids to get out.”

“Yeah, I’ll let him know. He’s a single dad too, lost his wife three years ago, so we try and get the kids together lots, you know.”

“Oh that’s sad… Yeah, it’ll be nice to get them all together then.” Cindy smiled. What a wonderful idea. She thought of the boys all playing together, Callum making new friends. Like she said, everything she did, she did it for him.

***

Chapter 5

Cindy added the final touched to her make up and admired herself in the full-length mirror. Jim had decided that the black dress looked smarter for the sort of do she was going to. His exact words were "you wanna blend in, look classy, not like a high-end hooker". He was probably right. The Dorchester was an elegant establishment and the event was a highsociety charity ball. So she went with chic. And if the night went well, she'd keep the red dress for future bookings.

The black still looked sexy though. She turned this way and that, admiring how well it hugged her curves. It looked good in the store, it looked even better now with her hair done and her make up on.

"Oh my God. Stunning." Jim's voice startled her and she turned to see him in the doorway. He leaned on the jamb with his arms crossed, drinking her in with his eyes. “Damn, if you weren’t going out…” He licked his lips and let his eyes do the talking. Cindy giggled. “I won’t lie, it’s nice to dress up.” She picked up her jewellery and Jim walked over to help her clasp the silver necklace behind her neck. He then placed his hands on her waist and stood behind her, watching in the mirror. “I’m in half a mind to keep you here…” Cindy laughed and twisted out of his grip, picking up her handbag.

“I didn’t have time to do Callum’s dinner.”

“It’s ok. I promised the little man McDonalds. Guys night out.” Jim winked at her. She smiled and pecked him quickly on the lips.

“Thank you babe.”

“Is that all I get?” Jim grabbed her wrist as she turned away and pulled her towards him.

“Hey, don’t mess up my make up now!” Cindy squealed.

“I won’t.” Jim smirked and ran his hands up and down her body, caressing her. He lifted the hem of her tight-fitting dress enough to slide a hand up her inner thigh.

Cindy tensed as his fingers touched her. He rubbed gently and a soft moan escaped her lips.

"Go get him, tiger." Jim whispered and pulled his hand away. He gave her butt a playful smack as he walked out of the room. Cindy stood there a moment adjusting herself. He's so naughty, she thought, smiling.

She checked herself one last time in the mirror and looked out of the window. A sleek black Mercedes was pulling up outside. She gasped.

"Oh wow…"

"Car's here babe!" Jim called from the lounge. Cindy shivered with anticipation. This would be a night to remember!

She tottered down the hallway and Jim put her black fake fur coat around her. Callum was watching TV.

"Bye baby, mummy's going to see you tomorrow. Be good for Jim ok?"

Callum nodded, barely moving his eyes from the screen. Jim opened the door for her.

"Make me proud babe." He lowered his voice.

"Remember, he's paid fifteen hundred up front, he needs to give you the rest." Cindy nodded and he brushed fluff off her coat. "And no drugs, ok?"

"Of course."

"Just cos these people are posh, doesn't mean they don't party. They've got the money for it. Watch him and watch your drinks, ok?"

"Yes babe, I know." She kissed him quickly, leaving a red mark on his lips. "See you tomorrow." Jim waggled his fingers at her as she left and Cindy made her way to the lift that had thankfully, finally been fixed that week. She shivered at the thought of tackling those endless, stinking stairs in her new heels.

Once at the bottom, she ignored the stares of the teenage estate boys hanging around the entrance and walked through with her head high. One of the wolf-whistled at her but she walked steadily, calmly towards the waiting car, knowing that their eyes were glued to her back. To her surprise, the driver got out, tipped his hat (he was actually wearing a chauffeur's hat like in the movies) and opened the back door for her.

"Thank you." Cindy said sweetly and as she turned to get in, she caught the astonished looks on the boys' faces. She winked, blew them a kiss and the driver shut the door. She grinned to herself behind the smoked glass windows and sat back on the leather seat. Her hand hit something beside her and she looked down. A small basket made into a tiny hamper was placed on the centre seat. It was wrapped with cellophane and a red ribbon and nestled inside on a bed of red shredded tissue paper was a small bottle of champagne and a crystal glass.

"With the compliments of Mr Harrison." She heard the driver say. He was smiling at her from the rear view mirror.

"For me?" Cindy asked. He nodded and started the engine.

"To get into the party mood." He said and drove off slowly. Cindy looked at the tiny hamper. It was adorable. She untied the silk ribbon and pulled out the bottle. Real champagne too. She didn't recognise the label which meant that is she hadn't ever come across it, it was bound to be expensive! She twisted the wire and the cork until it came off with a small pop.

Bubbles began to rise from the open mouth and she quickly grabbed the glass to pour it in.

"Oh sorry! I'm making a mess!" she exclaimed, holding the glass and bottle away from her to keep the dripping champagne off her dress.

"Not to worry. The valet will clean it." The driver replied, his attention on the road. "Enjoy."

Cindy got the bubbling drink under control, secured the half-empty bottle back in its hamper and sat back. She sipped her drink daintily, watching the streets of London go by. She felt like a queen.

***

Dusk had turned to night when the Merc joined the slow-moving queue of expensive cars lined up outside the Dorchester. Fairy lights adorned the winter shrubbery all along the front and the inside was bathed in a warm glow from the chandeliers hanging in the lobby.

Cindy composed herself as her heart began to beat and nerves threatened to take hold of her. Up ahead she could see people exiting their cars and limos. The men opened the doors for their dates, offering a hand for them to hold on to as they elegantly stepped out of the cars. Then the couples were greeted by the smiling doormen in their crisp uniforms and top hats, who opened the doors for them to vanish into the lavish interior.

She watched the ladies. How they walked, tall and erect, how they carried their purses and smiled gracefully to the people they greeted. She straighten her own back and practiced a small nod of the head and smile, mimicking what she observed. Their car crawled further forward, waiting for its turn to arrive at the drop-off point and she spotted a lone man in his late twenties standing out front.

That must be him, she thought. Everyone else was arriving in pairs, she hadn't seen anyone single come out of a car and he was the only man standing alone, waiting. She let her eyes take him in from the safety of her dark window. He wasn't too tall, just above average but tall enough for her. Sharply dressed in a tailored black suit with a thin silk trim on the hem and a black tie around his crisp white collar. His blonde hair had some length to it, probably chin-length but was slicked back in a tidy, orderly fashion. She couldn't see his eyes from where she sat but his jawline was square and his features chiselled. He didn't look at all nervous.

It always made the job a lot easier if the client was handsome and boy this guys was. Cindy realised she had stopped breathing and made a small gasping sound as she took a breath. The car moved on and suddenly it was her turn to get out. She gathered her purse and was about to open the door but the handsome young man had already walked over and was leaning in for the handle. She pasted the most elegant smile she could on her face and waited for the door to swing open.

"You must be Cindy." The young man beamed at her. "I'm Patrick. Welcome." He stepped aside and Cindy climbed out of the car as tidily as she could. Her smile stayed on her lips and as soon as she was out he stood straight and inclined her head in the way she had seen the other ladies do.

"Nice to meet you Patrick." She offered her hand and he surprised her by taking it and bringing it gently to his lips.

"A pleasure." He said after he kissed it. Cindy was speechless. She withdrew it politely and Patrick offered the crook of his elbow. "Shall we?"

"Oh. Of course." Cindy managed to mutter through her surprise and laced her arm through his own. Patrick smiled and led her past the grinning doormen, through the large doors and into a wonderland beyond her wildest dreams.

***

Patrick was a real gentleman. He introduced Cindy as his date and nobody asked any questions. If they suspected she was anything else, they had the decency to keep quiet. It was a crowd like Cindy had never been around before, well-spoken and dignified, polite and friendly. Patrick charmed everyone with his chatter and jokes and Cindy remained by his side throughout the evening, laughing alongside them and offering compliments to all the ladies they met. The champagne kept flowing, the food was delicious and the amounts of money pledged to the various charitable causes, vast.

By the end of the evening, she was having the time of her life and had all but forgotten that she was in fact, working. That realisation came back to her with a crash when Patrick whispered in her ear "I think it's time to go. My room is upstairs."

She smiled and nodded as they said their goodbyes and made their way out of the large ballroom. Patrick took her hand and walked slowly with her to the gleaming lifts. They got in and he inserted a key-card in a slot at the top, pressing the button beside it. The Terraced Penthouse.

"I should have told you earlier, but you look exquisite." He said in a low voice, stroking her face. Cindy knew this was her cue.

"We aim to please."

"Oh, I hope so." Patrick whispered and leaned in, brushing her lips with his. Cindy felt a tingling go through her. No one had ever kissed her like that before. It was... sensuous. She pushed forward an inch to kiss him back and he reciprocated, his hand stroking the small of her back. His lips were soft around hers, pressing gently, his tongue timidly exploring her mouth. When they broke away, Cindy's head spun. What was that feeling?

The lift stopped with a ping and Patrick stepped out backward, pulling her gently into the room. She followed like an obedient lamb, in a daze. His eyes never left her own and in the back of her mind she thought *Blue. That's their colour, blue like the ocean…* Patrick led her to the opulent bedroom, where a large, velvet-covered bed awaited. The lights were set low and fresh flowers spread their scent in the air.

Cindy remembered her role. She moved closer to him and unbuttoned his trousers. Her hand slid down the front.

"No." He surprised her by taking her wrist and pushing her hand away. "Let me." Cindy was confused. She was about to try again when he took her by the shoulders and turned her positioning her against the bed. He gently pushed and she lay down. Patrick pulled off her shoes, one at a time, kissing each leg as he did so. His hands then slid up her thighs, found her knickers and pulled slowly, all the way down until they fell to the floor. Cindy smiled and brought her knees up a little, exposing the pink flesh between her legs.

He smiled. His hands slid up the length of her legs again, caressing, kissing, then up her buttocks, pushing her dress up, along her sides and up her arms, taking the dress off in one long, sensual motion. He brought himself to his knees, looking down on her naked body, trailing a finger along her skin. Cindy's heart beat faster. He then bent down and began to kiss her neck, her breasts, her tummy, until his mouth found her soft, wet flesh and Cindy gasped with surprise and pleasure. His tongue slid in and out of her, around her clitoris, sending waves of pleasure rippling through her body.

"Oh... god..." she moaned, as he slid two fingers inside her, licking her at the same time. "Oh... god..." she continued, giving herself up to the sensation, rocking gently to the rhythm of his fingers sliding in and out, in and out while his tongue kept the pressure on. She had no idea how long it lasted, or how loud she was as she lost herself in a white light, riding the waves of real ecstasy for the first time in her life.

***

Chapter 6

Cindy stirred gently in the silk sheets, slowly drifting out of the deepest sleep she had ever had. She turned her head into the soft, down pillows, wondering vaguely where she was. This wasn't her bed… Then the night gradually came back to her, the pleasure Patrick and herself had shared…

She opened her eyes and saw him lying there beside her, on his back. His profile was as handsome in daylight as she remembered from the night before. His golden hair, now tousled, fell in messy strands around his head, giving him an oddly rugged appearance. She smiled. The men she slept with were just customers, ships passing in the night, but she felt an odd stirring inside for this one. He had treated her gently, unlike the rough and ready guys she had known and he had given her such pleasure as she had not experienced before, not even with Jim.

In fact, she had orgasmed twice… Once when he took her in his mouth, and then after, when he climbed on top of her for his turn, he had moved inside her with such passion, she had felt herself rise again towards a climax which came in shuddering waves at the same time as his own.

She moved her hand toward his face and gentry traced his profile, from forehead to lips, waking him. Patrick inhaled deeply and turned, his hand falling on her naked waist. His eyes opened and locked on to her own. She thought she would drown in the piercing blue that stared at her.

"Morning…" he muttered and stroked her side gently, his hands now slipping to her buttocks. His touch and the memory of her pleasure made Cindy pulsate with sudden anticipation. But she had to keep it professional. She smiled and raised herself on an elbow, moving away from his hand an inch.

"I have to go lover boy." She purred. Patrick pouted, reaching for her smooth buttock again.

"Don't I get a morning treat?" He stroked her, sliding his hand forward to stroke the fur on her mound. Cindy ached for him to take her again but she knew the score. Keep them wanting more, then the jobs come in.

She giggled and slid away, getting out of bed.

"Uh-uh sunshine. Night's over."

"Can I see you again?" His eyes were drinking her in, the same way he had done at the gala. "Let me take you to dinner?"

"You'll have to speak to the boss." Cindy was already puling on her dress. She reached for the envelope on the dresser and had a quick look at the wad of cash inside.

"It's all there." Patrick said. She felt a pang of embarrassment but pushed it aside and tucked the envelope in her bag. "I'll call you a car." Patrick added and reached for the phone on his side of the bed.

Cindy went to the bathroom and freshened herself up while he sorted out her transport when she came out, he was in his boxers, waiting. She smiled, slightly awkward, and he approached her casually.

"Surely one last kiss is included in the package?" he smiled down at her and she almost shivered. She raised her mouth to his and his lips closed around hers in a languishing kiss that made her knees go weak. When they broke away, there was lust in his eyes and Cindy could feel his pressing against her, hard again.

"One more date?" he whispered, swallowing his desire. Cindy's breath caught in her throat as she tried to answer.

"Whatever you want…" she managed to mutter and mercifully he nodded and stepped back to let her go.

"And this time, you stay for breakfast too. That's the deal." He stated and Cindy could only nod and smile. She grabbed her shoes and as calmly as she could, she eft the bedroom and out of the penthouse.

All through the ride home she couldn't help returning to Patrick's face, his lips on her own, his tongue between her legs. She caught herself grinning like a schoolgirl a few times and had to press her head to the window, pretending to look outside and keep her face hidden from the driver's curious eyes in the rearview mirror. Of course he know why she had been there. They always did.

She actually breathed with relief when they pulled up outside the council block and she hurried out and into the lobby. Rain had started to fall and she was thankful for it, as no youths were loitering outside to wolf whistle at her or make snarky remarks. She got in the lift and went up to the flat.

Jim was cooking a massive fry-up breakfast and beaming from ear to ear when she walked in. The smell of bacon hit her and she suddenly realised she was famished.

“Ah babe, well timed, I’m starving!” She exclaimed and Jim put his tongs down, strode over to her and effortlessly lifted her in a bear hug.

“You killed it babe! You really did!” He twirled her around and Cindy had to beg him through her giggles to set her down. “I don’t know what you did but man, he’s already called me and booked again!” Cindy’s heart fluttered and she brought her hands to her mouth to cover the sudden grin that spread on her face. Luckily, Jim mistook it for surprise.

"Friday night. He needs a dinner date apparently. You spend the night again and he's offering extra for the morning too..." He chuckled. "These rich guys babe" he waved the tongs at her "all the money in the world but lonely as fuck." He plated up the bacon and cracked eggs in the pan. "Literally paying just to have someone eat with them." He shook his head laughing. "Did you get the rest of the money?"

"Of course." Cindy said and pulled the envelope from her bag. He took it from her and counted it while waiting for the eggs to cook.

"I'm going to take a quick shower and get changed. Don't want to get the dress dirty." Cindy said and made her way down the corridor to the bathroom. Jim chuckled from the kitchen.

"Sweetheart, with this kinda money you can get all the dresses you want!" He called to her but she was already shutting the door behind her. I'd rather save it and put it to good use, she thought. She had never planned to be a sex worker, it had been Jim's idea and the money had of course been welcome. But Cindy knew she could do better. Her night with Patrick had opened her mind to a new world of possibilities that she had not thought of before.

With the escorting work, she would make a hundred times more with each job and wouldn't have to sleep with nearly as many men as she did before. She could save up and maybe begin to look at a real future for her and Callum. She would have to talk to Jim, he wouldn't let her give up the job easily but with the money she could take a course in something, learn some skills, make an honest living with a real job. She was still young.

She let her mind wander as she fantasized in the shower about her future. A little house, terraced maybe with a garden for Callum to play in. She could get him a swing set and a slide and a paddling pool for the summer. She saw herself, kissing him goodbye at the school gates, in her work uniform, a nurse maybe or a beautician. She could even learn how to drive and get a little car, so they wouldn't have to get soaked at bus stops anymore. The possibilities were endless.

***

And all of it achievable, by simply pleasing one client, maybe two, who had the right amount of money to spend. Patrick's face appeared in her mind again and she sighed. Friday couldn't come quickly enough.

After breakfast, Jim pecked her on the cheek and told her to take the day to relax, maybe do some more shopping. It wouldn't do to turn up at her next expensive date in the same dress, even if it was a different colour. He pressed a thousand pounds cash in her hand and pinched her bottom, laughing. "Treat yourself" he had said, "this is yours to keep." When he left, Cindy put two hundred in her purse and hid the rest in an old handbag in her closet. She would be frugal and start saving now.

She spent the rest of the day at the shopping centre, avoiding the designer shops and finding some tasteful and elegant bargains that were just as good looking as the fancy dresses she had bought. At 3.20 she picked up Callum from school and treated him with dinner at his favourite little café on the corner, complete with ice cream and brownies for dessert. His chocolatecovered grin made it all worthwhile and she sat watching him devour his food lovingly.

***

It was gone 11pm when Jim returned, slamming the front door angrily behind him. Cindy was watching TV in the living room and jumped up, rushing to see what was the matter. Luckily Callum was a deep sleeper and didn't stir in his room.

"Jim?" She whispered down the corridor, after checking Callum's room. "You ok?" Jim's bulky frame was outlined in the light coming through the glass on the front door. He stormed past her into the living room, throwing his coat on an armchair and falling on the sofa with a grunt. Cindy followed, waiting. Jim had a temper and if he'd been in an argument with someone, he could be in one of his moods…

Eventually he spoke. "That asshole Mark… He's been messing me around…" He sighed heavily and shook his head "it's ok, not for you to worry. Just business stuff."

Cindy nodded but could tell he was really wound up. Sure enough, his eyes moved to her and he said

"Callum asleep?"

Cindy nodded. Jim smiled and patted the sofa next to him with a wink. "Close the door." Cindy did so and moved towards him. "I could use some stress relief…" he smirked, already unbuttoning his trousers. "You got something to help Big Jim?" he pulled out his erection and Cindy knew there was no refusing now. If he went into one of his rages he would wake Callum and she didn't want that…

She knelt in front of him and Jim groaned loudly as she took him in her mouth. He grabbed her head and pulled it closer, moving his hips up and down. Cindy worked on him for a few minutes, turning her mind blank. As his moans got louder, he suddenly yanked her head up and pushed her onto the sofa. Without complaint she drew her legs up just as he moved on top of her and penetrated her in one quick movement. She gasped a little at the sudden invasion but soon he was sliding in and out of her with hard and fast thrusts.

She closed her eyes and let him release his anger. His hips ground against her inner thighs as he pounded her, every thrust meeting her pelvis with a loud slapping sound, his hard penis ruthlessly ramming inside her. She felt nothing but the dull sensation of having sex, wet flesh slipping on wet flesh, nothing akin to the satisfaction Patrick had given her. Jim's thrusting became faster and faster until with one almighty shudder he came, pushing hard against her as he groaned in animal pleasure. He flopped on her, squashing her with his weight into the cushions.

"God I needed that..." he panted in her ear. She stroked his back and kissed his shoulder.

"Better now?" She murmured. In reply he buried his sweaty face in her neck and groaned with satisfaction.

Cindy stroked his hair softly, but in her mind was a golden halo of messy tufts laying on a feather down pillow...

***

Chapter 7

Friday felt like a lifetime away and the week dragged on for Cindy. Her upcoming booking with Patrick had done little to quell Jim's temper after that weekend; he had further fallen out with his business partner, over what Cindy didn't know and didn't care, but it had put him in a foul mood all week. Even the prospect of the five grand Patrick was paying for Cindy's company didn't dissuade him from squeezing as much money as he could from her.

She had implored him to give her the week off, but didn't push it, fearing his anger may turn dangerous. She'd seen him beat a grown man before and although he had never hit her, he could become violent and nasty in other ways.

And what if he took his anger out on Callum? He'd already snapped at the poor boy a couple of times that week. He was quick to apologise and came home with sweets for him, but Cindy saw his temper was wearing thin and it didn't take much for him to lose it… So she swallowed her pride, kept Callum busy and in the evenings went to the parties he had found for her. She lay back, bent over or knelt for every guy he sent her to and bided her time patiently until Friday finally arrived.

She had had to bribe Callum with every promise she could think of for the weekend. The boy had almost thrown a tantrum when she said she had to go out again, and she was anxious about leaving her fractious son with an already fractious Jim. She bought him a new box of Lego and his favourite ice cream to have after dinner, reminding him that they would be going to the fun fair with Logan at the weekend.

“You can go on all the rides you want, as many times as you want.” She promised. “And we’ll get candy floss and hot dogs and stay as long as you want to.” Relief had washed over her at his happy face and she made him promise in turn to be a good boy and listen to Jim.

Jim himself was in a slightly better mood when he saw her out.

“Make sure he pays half upfront, ok babe?” he muttered. “And keep him keen. I can use the money right now.”

“Ok, Jim.” She said meekly and left for the car that was waiting for her. It was a different driver who held the door open for her this time but the same mini hamper welcomed her on the back seat. She smiled and poured herself the champagne, trying to still her heart that had started fluttering.

The drive was shorter than last time. The car rolled through the traffic on Kensington High Street and turned down a narrow side road, moving away from the crowded shopping area towards a quiet street lined with elegant town houses and well-pruned trees. Cindy saw light pouring from a small restaurant front onto the pavement, where Patrick stood waiting under the burgundy canopy. She took a breath and smiled.

He was dressed in a well cut dinner suit, his hair glowing under the soft light. The car pulled over outside and he open the door for her with a genuine smile on his face.

“Milady.” He bowed and Cindy giggled. He straightened up with a twinkle in his eye. “It has been a long week” he sighed and offered his hand. Cindy took it and stepped out of the car as elegantly as she could. The car drove off and they were left standing face to face, alone, in the golden pool of light on the dark street.

“It’s a pleasure to see you again.” Patrick said and kissed her lightly on the lips. Cindy’s heart drummed in her chest and she fought to control herself. She felt her cheeks flush.

“Thank you. Pleasure to see you too.” She suddenly remembered the money and groaned inside. It was easy asking the usual horny boys to pay upfront, but with Patrick it just felt tactless. She kept the smile on her face while she scrabbled to find a way to say it. But as she groped for the right words, Patrick’s hand reached into his pocket and discreetly slipped an envelope into her handbag.

Cindy almost melted. He really was a gentleman in every way. Or was he simply trying to hide his own embarrassment? Whatever the reason, she was grateful for his careful action. She smiled sweetly at him.

“Shall we?” she cooed.

“Yes. I’m famished.” Patrick said and opened the door for her to step inside. The smells hit Cindy first – garlic and charcoal and spices filled the air but not in the overwhelming way she was used to. Somehow the aromas that drifted from the kitchen added to the atmosphere of the opulent interior, like a perfume on a silk dress. There was none of the cloying stench of grease and sweat she was accustomed to in her local diner.

The interior was softly lit by warm overhead lights hanging over each table and classical music played in the background. Well-dressed and wellmannered groups and couples sat talking sipping their drinks and dabbing the mouths elegantly with the thick cotton napkins on their laps. Again, Cindy took note of each gesture as they walked through the restaurant to the table, led by a uniformed waiter.

Their table was tucked away in a private corner, away from the crowd, in a romantic nook lit mostly by candles. Patrick pulled her chair out for her and then sat opposite her. The waiter handed them the menus and recommended various bottles of wine that Cindy had never heard of.

“You know I trust your judgement, Pierre” Patrick laughed. “Bring us a white and a red, you choose.” Pierre nodded his head with a proud smile.

“Very well Mr Harrison. I know just what you will like. New delivery today of an excellent vintage.” He bowed and left.

“The wine here is really good.” Patrick told Cindy. She smiled.

“I can’t say I am an expert.”

“Maybe we need to spend more time together” Patrick winked. Her heart did a little flutter again and this time she really did feel herself blush. Did he notice?

When Pierre arrived with the wines, Patrick tried both and chose the red for their meal. He then asked Pierre to send two bottles of each to the penthouse he was staying in and ordered their finest steaks for dinner.

The wine was indeed excellent, the best Cindy had ever tasted. But that was not saying much, when it was usually Tesco’s own brand or whatever offer

Jim found. After two glasses she was giddy and the evening passed in a blur of endless conversation, laughter and heavenly food.

Sometime during their meal, Patrick had moved to the seat beside her and his hand was now creeping up her thigh. Cindy, fuelled by good wine and the prospect of another heavenly night with his attentions, leaned in and kissed him passionately. Patrick reciprocated and his tongue pated her lips, exploring her wine-favoured mouth. Cindy moaned with unexpected pleasure and they parted slowly, Patrick looking deep into her eyes.

His hand found the top of her thigh and pushed against her already wet knickers. "I think it's time to get the bill…" he whispered and Cindy nodded, her own hand stroking his thigh gently. He had to move out of her reach, laughing.

"Not here, gorgeous…"

Cindy giggled at the thought of him walking past the posh diners with an erection pushing against his trousers. "Hurry up then, lover boy…" she purred and he rushed over to the concierge.

In a couple of minutes they were in the back of a car, driving to Patrick's hotel. His hand had not left her inner thigh all during the drive and Cindy had had to really control her expression as his fingers moved in tiny circles on her soft mound, send her heart into palpitations.

Somehow they made it through the hotel lobby gracefully and into the lift to the penthouse. The doors had barely slid shut when Patrick pushed her back onto the wall and sealed her lips in a deep, passionate kiss, his fingers finding exactly the right spot to press on between her legs. City finally let herself go and moaned with such pleasure, he had to pull back and look at her.

"Oh, you like this, huh?" he whispered and she couldn't help herself nodding. His fingers pressed harder.

"Yes…" she sighed, closing her eyes "yes…"

Patrick kissed her again, working his fingers in a rhythm that threatened to send her into madness. Back and forth, then around and back and forth again. Cindy began involuntarily to grind against them.

The elevator pinged and he pulled away abruptly.

“Not yet, gorgeous…” he teased, leaving her panting against the wall. The doors opened and he stepped backwards out of the lift, pulling her gently by the hand. She followed like a puppy, breathing heavily, obediently. Patrick continued to walk backwards, his eyes locked onto hers, leading her to the large bedroom. He stopped by the bed and pulled her close to him, pressing his lips to hers. Cindy was lost again in a sea of passion, feeling his hands travel up and down her back, then down to her waist, hips, thighs…

His fingers tugged at the hem of her dress and, still kissing her, slowly pulled it up and Cindy raised her arms for it to go over her head. He dropped it on the floor and brought his lips to her neck, kissing and nibbling as he fingers expertly worked on her bra clasp. He pulled it off and looked down at the breasts, firm and pert. He lowered himself and took one dark nipple into his mouth, sucking gently. Cindy tilted her head back and moaned, her fingers tangled in his long hair.

His hands that were on her back pressing her to his face, slid down and pulled her lacy knickers off. He caressed her legs as he came up, stopping at her tight buttocks, squeezing one each in his hands. He kissed her breasts and slid down to her belly, planting soft kisses on her skin as he went along, moving lower, closer to her vagina.

"Hello there…" he whispered and his tongue began to explore her soft crevices again, making Cindy's legs buckle.

"Oh….." she moaned loudly and Patrick continued his tonguing while at the same time pushing her gently backwards onto the bed. Cindy lay back and raised her legs. Her hand dug into his scalp as she pushed him harder onto her, willing his tongue to go deeper, breathing now coming in small hitched gasps.

"Yes… yes… oh…." She panted and began to move her hips in small circles to meet the pressure of his tongue. "Oh god… yes…." Just as she felt the brink of an orgasm coming, Patricks tongue came away and moved up her belly, to her breasts.

“Not yet, gorgeous…” he teased again.

“Please…” Cindy moaned and he smirked, working his tongue around each nipple as his hand came down to unfasted his trousers. Cindy’s fingers fumbled with his shirt buttons and in seconds she had pulled it off. She kissed his toned, hairless chest and nibbled his neck. Patrick pushed his trousers down and lay naked above her, resting on his elbows, his hard penis a hair’s breadth from her skin. Cindy reached for it and he moved it aside playfully.

“Oh, you want something?” He asked. Cindy raised her head and kissed him hungrily, grasping his hips. He reciprocated and let her guide him inside her. Cindy gasped with pleasure, feeling the hard thickness of his member slide up inside her dripping pussy. She moaned with delight as he pushed himself fully in, his size filling her up completely.

“Oh God!” she shouted, lifting her hips to push harder against him. Patrick began to move in and out, fully pushing inside her, every thrust gentle and calculated. He moved his own hips in circles and her own came up to meet him, both moving in unison, in a private dance that sent Cindy’s mind reeling. This was real sex. Real pleasure from a man who worked hard to give it to her.

She continued to grind her hips on his, gasping with every thrust. His breathing also became faster, as did his rhythm. Cindy closed her eyes and let their bodies work together, giving and receiving, her pleasure accelerating as his hard-on slipped in and out of her, finding all her pleasure points. She felt herself reach the edge of orgasm again and from his rapid breathing, sensed that Patrick was also nearing his. She released herself to the sensation and his hands suddenly grabbed her buttocks and pulled her hard on to him as he pushed his throbbing climax into her. With loud moans of pleasure, they came simultaneously, Cindy's legs clasped tight around his back, as the waves of her orgasm rippled through her entire body.

Chapter 8

Once again Cindy slept deeply, completely spent after her night of passion. When the morning sun began to creep through the silk curtains of the penthouse bedroom, she stretched and rolled on to her side, feeling refreshed and invigorated. Patrick lay on his back, his profile outlined by the soft morning light. She watched him for a while, sleeping peacefully, his chest rising and falling gently.

She had never in her life had sex with anyone who had given her such pleasure. She thought she had, with the few boyfriends who'd treated her well, but now she had experienced what real pleasure was, she realised how blind she had been. Sex to her had been mostly a chore, one she had told herself she had liked, even with Jim. She did like pleasuring Jim, after all he did for her she did want to do something for him in return and it made her feel good that she could.

But now a slow realisation was creeping in. She was just paying him back. Or maybe he was paying her. With his home and his protection, in exchange for her body. Maybe Jim was nothing more than the countless men who banged her and paid for the privilege.

Paid Jim. Not her. Pieces of her life's puzzle were suddenly starting to fall into place and Cindy was becoming torn. But the truth she had avoided for so long had finally hit home. She was a prostitute. Nothing more to it. She could keep telling herself she was doing it because she liked it, because it was just a job she was good at, but the truth hung there in the forefront of her mind like a beacon. She was nothing more than a cheap whore, and her supposed boyfriend was a pimp.

She sighed. Callum's giggling face appeared in front of her. Of course she did it all for him. Sure, she could keep telling herself that, but was that all she could do for him? Couldn't she do better? *Keep him keen*, Jim's words echoed in her head. She watched Patrick's beautiful face. He was not like the others. He was… a giver. She smiled. If she was going to be a whore, well she may as well work her way to the top. Wasn't that how it worked? She raised her hand and trailed her finger softly along his skin. Cindy knew she would have no problem keeping this one keen. She liked him too.

Patrick stirred.

"Good morning…" She whispered and kissed him softly on the shoulder. Patrick smiled in his sleep and his hand came up to hers. He took it and brought it to his lips.

"Morning…" He muttered, still half asleep. Cindy moved closer and kissed his neck, her lips hovering by his ear.

"Sleep well?" she whispered, caressing his chest and moving her hand lower down. Patrick nodded and suddenly let out a soft moan. Cindy smiled "oh, well someone else is up too…" she kissed him on the lips and slipped her leg over his body, straddling him while her had stroked his already hard penis. Patrick stretched and smiled.

"Mmmm.... That's nice..." he muttered, eyes still closed. Cindy positioned herself over his morning erection and slowly slid down on it. "Oooohhh...." Patrick groaned. Cindy let her own weight settle her onto him and felt his tip reach deep inside her. "Aaah..." she exhaled with delight. Patrick's hips pushed up and she placed her palms on his chest, rocking her hips back and forth as he bounced her gently. His hands came to her waist and soon they were rocking to a perfect rhythm again. Cindy could feel every inch of him inside her. She dug her nails into his chest and moved her body more urgently, her vagina tight around his penis. She felt herself begin to lose control as his movement also became more rapid.

"Yes... yes..." they both panted, as their pleasure escalated. One of Patrick's hands came off Cindy's waist and slid expertly between her legs, finding her clitoris. The sudden stimulation sent a lightning bolt through her and she came hard, screaming with ecstasy. Patrick followed suit, pushing his hips up and lifting her off the bed as he emptied himself inside her.

They stayed in that pulsating nirvana for a moment, then Cindy flopped on his chest panting. Then she started giggling. Patrick's hand ran down her back, stroking her.

"What's so funny?" his breathless voice was in her ear. She kept giggling and he pushed up with his hips, his semi-hard cock still inside her. "Oi!" he chuckled and Cindy gasped. She wiggled her hips a little and it was his turn to gasp.

"I've never screamed before" she laughed, still wiggling her hips.

"Well done *me* then, huh?! Patrick said and gasped again "oh that's nice… I think I'm getting hard again…"

Cindy's eyes widened in surprise. Who *was* this guy!? She continued to rotate her hips a bit more and sure enough she felt his erection fill her innermost spaces again. To her surprise, she felt her own pleasure heighten once more.

"Well, aren't you a surprise?" she muttered and kissed him passionately. Patrick's tongue found hers and he pushed his mouth on hers, at the same time rolling her over so he was on top.

"It's all you, gorgeous..." he moved gently deeper inside her "you work magic on me." He kissed her again and Cindy moaned, laying in the soft sheets. They moved slowly this time, already spent but willing.

They kissed, caressed and met each other softly, slowly building back up to another, sweeter climax.

Breakfast was delivered on a silver trolley and laid out on the penthouse balcony. It was a rare, clear and bright London morning and they sat in their plush robes eating waffles and strawberries with fresh orange juice. Cindy was famished from their exertions and by the look of it so was Patrick. They said little while they ate but the smiles Patrick gave her were genuine. Cindy's heart fluttered and she felt a tinge of sadness when she saw the time.

"I've got to head back, I'm sorry." She said and she meant it. Money or no money, she would have loved to have spent the whole day with him. The thought of his hands on her made her shiver with the memory of their lovemaking. Patrick nodded. Did she detect a hint of regret in his eyes just then? He chewed his lip for a moment.

"I'll call for a car." He said finally, and Cindy was disappointed at the dryness of his tone. She had expected him to mention another date, but he had been quiet most of their breakfast. She nodded with a tightlipped smile and went inside to get changed.

When she was ready, Patrick saw her to the elevator door. He stood silently beside her while they waited. The lift pinged and the doors slid open. Cindy waited for a heartbeat for him to say something and when he didn't, she stepped in.

"I know I shouldn't probably say this, but…" she couldn't stop herself "I had a really nice time with you Patrick." She smiled. "Goodbye."

His eyes came up to meet hers as the doors slid shut. Just before they closed, he jammed his hand in the way, forcing them open again and making Cindy jump.

"I had a really good time too." He blurted. "Really, really good." Their eyes were locked onto each other's. Cindy waited, her heart beating with anticipation. Patrick swallowed. "Look, I don't know if this is possible, but…" he fumbled for words. *Another date, thank goodness,* Cindy thought with relief.

"I would like to arrange for… an exclusive engagement. If possible?"

Cindy's heart nearly leapt out of her chest.

"Exclusive…?" she managed to utter.

"Yes." Patrick nodded. He stepped closer to her, locking the doors open.

"I… I would have to speak to my… manager…" Cindy stuttered. She knew Jim would say no. One client alone was not profitable.

"I understand there may be a… higher cost" Patrick said, stroking her face. His fingers carried on down the length of her arm and he took her hand in his. "You see… I like you Cindy. And I'm not used to not getting what I like…" He grinned like a petulant little boy and Cindy couldn't help but giggle.

"I like you too…" she whispered and instantly regretted it, embarrassed. She sounded like a little schoolgirl. Patrick pulled her close and kissed her lightly.

"So let's work something out." He whispered in her ear.

***

All through the car journey, Cindy played and replayed the words in her mind, how she would present Patrick's proposal to Jim. She would have to catch him in a good mood too. She knew he would object straight away. But she also knew how to work him. Eventually, he would agree, at least to Patrick's eyes. Obviously when she would be back home there would be nothing stopping him fitting in other clients or a party if he found one, He'd find ways to make more money out of her.

The thought disgusted her for the first time ever. She had tasted pleasure, respect and why not – happiness. Patrick liked her. And she had a feeling that he did not mean just sexually. Sure they had the most mind blowing sex but hadn't they also enjoyed each other's company at dinner and breakfast? She remembered the delicious food, the luxurious surroundings, the size of the strawberries alone! Callum loved strawberries, if only he could have seen them!

Her heart melted at the thought of her son. She longed to see him and hold him, and spoil him rotten, just the way she had been. Yes, Cindy had glimpsed a new reality, and suddenly her own now seemed shabby and joyless… What kind of future was she building for her son? Drug parties and trafficking with Jim? Was that where she wanted Callum to end up?

Her resolve was set by the time the car dropped her off. She would confront Jim, persuade him to take Patrick's offer. She would comply with his few dealings on the side if she had to, but Patrick would be her one and only regular client. She would ensure he took up most of her bookings and she would continue to save her cut until there was enough to move out. A crystal clear awareness had settled in her mind. She did not love Jim, or need him. And he did not love her. They had a business arrangement and that was all.

This last part of course she wouldn't disclose to Jim. No. Patrick would be her way out, but as far as Jim would know, he was just a well-paying client. Just another rich guy getting what he wanted. Well, if that worked for guys like him, Cindy would make it work for her too. She would get what she wanted, and get herself out of the shitty existence Jim had her trapped in...

***

Chapter 9

"He'll have to pay a hell of a lot more if he wants exclusivity." Jim wagged a finger in Cindy's face. "You better not have said yes!" She shrank away from it – he was almost jabbing her now.

"Jim, calm down!" she tried to control her own temper. It wouldn't do to aggravate him further He was still in his mood. She sweetened her voice. "I'm just telling what he said. Don't shoot the messenger babe…" she pushed his hand aside gently and walked toward Callum's room, wagging her behind for good measure. "Just think about it. It's good money." She turned and flashed a vixen smile at him before going into Callum's room. "Hey baby, ready to go to the fair?" she cooed at her boy who leapt in her arms as soon as he saw her. Jim stood in the living room for a moment, then stomped down the hall.

"Cindy!"

She felt Callum flinch in her arms at his bellowing voice and a primal rage surged inside her.

How dare he… How dare he raise his voice in front of her child… Jim's form filled the doorframe and he crossed his muscular arms. Cindy kissed Callum's head and held back the rising anger. "Go get your shoes baby. And your coat, it's chilly out." Callum beamed and Cindy shot Jim a warning look. Jim said nothing and moved aside for the boy to squeeze past him. He may have been the man in that house, but even he knew not to mess with Cindy where her son was concerned. She glared at him.

"You raise your voice at me like that in front of him again and I'm out of here." She hissed at him. It was a bluff, her go-to threat that both knew meant nothing, but it served to remind Jim her boundaries. He could do what he wanted with her, but her child was sacred. And it didn't hurt for him to remember where his money came from. Jim's anger abated a fraction and he dropped his voice. It wasn't any softer.

"What did you promise him?"

"Nothing. I told you, He wants me exclusively, he knows it will cost more. He'll pay."

"I had other customers lined up. Bankers. Politicians! We could make ten times more than one client."

Cindy shuddered inside. So Jim the businessman had spent his time wisely, lining up goodness knew how many creeps willing to pay for her body. He cared nothing for her. She swallowed her anger again.

"Like I said, just passing on the message. You're the business brains, figure it out. But I'm telling you, I've been with this guy, seen how he spends, "she cast her hook "I don't think any price is too high." She watched Jim take the bait, hook line and sinker.

"You think so?"

"Oh I know so." She smiled, knowing she had him where she wanted. She slinked past him, brushing her hand across his crotch as she did so "and you know I can keep him keen..." she said suggestively. She carried on down the corridor to Callum who was struggling with his broken coat zip. A sly smile crept along Jim's face.

"I guess I can negotiate some terms with him." He said. Cindy zipped up Callum's coat and got hers off the hook.

"You do that babe. You're the brains, right?" She flashed another sweet smile, feeling victorious inside. "I'm talking Callum to the fair, see you later." She took Callum's hand and left with him skipping and chatting beside her all the way.

***

Becky and Logan were waiting at the park entrance when they arrived. The boys ran to each other and the girls embraced.

"You look... different..." Becky remarked, holding Cindy at arm's length.

"Really?" Cindy said and Becky examined her face.

"Yeah, you're like... glowing."

Cindy giggled. Becky raised an eyebrow. "And you're... giggling..? Come on girl, spill it!"

Cindy shook her head about to say it's nothing, but Callum's voice saved her from trying to explain herself. "Mummy!!! CAN WE GET CANDYFLOSS?" he yelled from across the lawn, pointing at the colourful cart strategically placed near the entrance. She rolled her eyes at Becky.

"I've promised him he can have anything he wants... This could be fun..." Becky smiled back and they walked to the boys who were jumping up and down around the cart. Cindy bought candy floss for both, refusing Becky's money. "No, it's ok, my treat."

"Ok, thank you, Logan, say thank you to Cindy."

The words barely left his mouth as he was already stuffing the pink fluff into it. Cindy and Becky laughed. It was nice to be out, and to see the kids having fun. They continued into the fair, chatting and running after each boy as they flew like bees from one stall to another. They put them on the little train ride for kids and stood aside watching them round and round in hoots of laughter as it went up and down its tracks.

"So… you think I'm gonna let you get away with not telling me what's going on?" Becky nudged Cindy. "I don't think I've seen you this happy before."

Cindy smiled and chewed her lip. Becky was her best friend. She hadn't told her everything about her life of course, she didn't have to, but she could share some things.

"Well….?" Becky leaned in front of her. "Now' the time, while they're busy!" she jabbed her thumb at the boys on the train. Cindy couldn't stop the grin splitting her face.

"I kinda… met someone…"

"You met someone?" Becky was confused. "What about Jim?"

Cindy shook her head. "Jim and I are not…" she didn't know how to put it. "I mean we were… but… we sort of have an arrangement."

Becky nodded. "Oh, ok. I get it. I thought you were a couple."

"We have been. It's just… well it's complicated."

"Honey, trust me, I get complicated. Say no more."

Cindy filled with warmth. At the moment she loved Becky like she'd never loved any friends before. A real friend, no judgement.

"But, do tell me about this guy!" Becky added. "I still want to hear the good stuff!" she put her arm around her "you know whatever you tell me stays with me right?"

"Yeah I know" Cindy hugged her back. The train ride was coming to an end. "So, his name is Patrick and he's kinda… hot."

Becky gasped with excitement.

"And minted…" Becky's eyes widened. "I mean, *minted.*" Cindy emphasised. "Like penthouse apartments minted." Becky began to flap her hands.

"Where did you meat this guy? I need to know more!" The boys were being helped off their cart by the ride operator, so she leaned in conspiratorially. "And… have you…?"

Cindy's look said it all and Becky melted with a sigh. "Oh god girl, we need to talk about this over over wine!"

"That sounds like a plan!" Cindy agreed. They collected the children and walked on to the next rides. Becky's phone buzzed in her pocket.

"Oh, it's my cousin, they're here" she said when she checked it. She looked around, but it was Logan who spotted them.

"Mummy, it's Tom! It's Tom and Uncle Malcolm!" he jumped up and down on the spot and shot off towards a man and a young boy about the same age. Becky waved them over. Cindy smiled politely, keeping an eye on Callum who stood shyly next to her now that his friend had left him. The man approached and hugged Becky.

"This is my friend Cindy, I told you about. This is my cousin, Malcolm." She introduced them.

"Nice to meet you." Malcolm smiled and they shook hands. He was taller than Becky but not by much, and was wrapped in an old brown coat and scarf. His hair was tucked under a woolly hat and his round glasses added the final touch to his "nerdy dad" appearance. "And this is?" he said, kneeling down to Callum's height.

"Oh," Cindy said. "This is my son Callum. Him and Logan are in the same class."

"Hello young man" Malcolm said and offered his hand. Callum shrank back a little into Cindy. "Ah, maybe a high five then?" Malcolm grinned and raised his hand. Callum grinned and smacked it hard with his. "Callum! Gentle!" Cindy scolded him.

"It's ok" Malcolm said "That was a big boy's high five, right?" he winked at Callum. "Now, has your friend abandoned you?" his voice turned authoritative. "Logan! Come introduce your friend to your cousin!"

he called over his shoulder and the boys ran over giggling. Within seconds, Callum had joined them and the three were running ahead like they had known each other for years. The adult followed behind, making small talk and keeping an eye on them.

Becky told Malcom about how Cindy and she had met at the school and they spoke about the children mostly. Cindy learned that Malcolm's wife had sadly passed away when Tom was a baby, so he too was a single parent like them. Becky and he often shared babysitting duties especially during half terms when they would arrange their shifts so they could have the kids on separate days while the other had to work.

"It's tough to juggle" Malcolm said "we all help each other how we can."

"Cindy has been a great help too, you've had Logan around a few afternoons when I had to work. I've managed to pick up some more shifts that way."

"That's really nice of you. "Malcolm said. "So what do you do, Cindy?"

"Oh, I… not much. My partner is a… trader."

"I thought you said you worked nights?" Becky piped up. Cindy backtracked.

"Oh, yeah. Sometimes. I help with the... business. They... pack orders overnight for next day shipments."

Becky and Malcolm nodded. Her lie seemed to make sense and they didn't ask more. Ahead, the boys were calling from the hot dog stand.

"Well, I guess it *is* dinner time..." Malcolm said and trotted up to them. "My treat!" he said pulling his wallet out. Cindy followed with Becky, feeling a little embarrassed. She didn't like lying to her best friend. But if she knew what she did, she might not want to be around her anymore, or let her child be around her. And Cindy wouldn't blame her. She sensed that Becky had not quite swallowed her story about night-packing, but she thankfully wasn't saying anything. Still, the lie burnt inside Cindy.

Malcolm bought them all hot dogs and they spent the rest of the afternoon treating the kids to everything they wanted, until it got dark. Malcolm had a hard time extracting Tom from his cousin and his new friend, but eventually managed to lead him away with promises of arranging playdates and meeting again. They waited with them at the bus stop and waved them off as it pulled away, leaving Becky and Cindy with the boys to walk the short distance back home.

"So, how about that wine?" Becky said in the silence. "It's Saturday night, and I've got nothing to do." She raised an eyebrow at Cindy. "Girls' night?"

Cindy was about to refuse – she didn't want to leave Callum alone with Jim for a second night in a row.

But Logan piped up.

"Can Callum have a sleepover mummy?" Can he?"

"Can I?" Callum added, turning to his mum. The women stopped and thought about it.

"I don't see why not." Becky said. "You can both stay!" she winked at Cindy "Then you can tell me all about your news…" she smirked and Cindy found herself smiling back.

"Ok, we'll go home and get our stuff and we'll see you in a bit then."

Callum and Logan shrieked with joy and he bounced all the way back to the flat. Cindy was prepared to argue with Jim again but luckily he was out. She packed an overnight bag for the two of them and wrote a note for Jim. *Sleepover at Becky's - don't stay up, see you in the morning.* She added a couple of x's as an afterthought. *Keep the peace*, she thought, and left the note on the kitchen table. She hurried Callum out, not wanting to bump into him if he was on the way back.

A girls' night sounded great and her awkward feeling from earlier began to lift. Becky was a good friend. She deserved an honest friend and so Cindy decided to open up to her more, test the waters and see if she could tell her the truth.

She needed someone to listen. The last week it had all been bubbling up inside her and now she knew without a doubt that she had been living in a lie. Who better to talk to but her best friend?

***

Chapter 10

The wine flowed late into the night after the boys went to bed and the girls loosened up. They sat with their legs curled under them on the soft carpet, their backs leaning on the sofa. In hushed tones punctuated by bursts of laughter and giggles, Cindy recounted her two dates with Patrick, while Becky listened attentively. Without going into too much detail, Cindy painted a good picture of how attentive he was to her sexual needs...

Becky sighed.

"Oh girl, he sounds dreamy..."

"You have no idea." Cindy smiled into her glass.

"And you said he was minted too?"

Cindy nodded. Becky exhaled loudly and topped up their glasses. "So where does a girl from the council block meet a rich guy from Dreamland?"

Cindy hesitated. She wanted to tell Becky everything. This was it...

"Well…" she began. "So, here's the thing, there's something I have wanted to tell you…" her eyes pleaded with her "but promise not to judge me?"

"Sweetheart." Becky sat up straight. "Who am I to judge anyone?" She put a hand on Cindy's arm and squeezed gently. "You know you can tell me anything, right?"

Cindy nodded. Her head turned towards the hallway, where the stairs led up to the room the boys were sleeping in. "You'd do anything for Logan, wouldn't you?"

"Would I? Girl, you know it."

"Same. For Callum. Everything I have done has been to keep him safe." Cindy's eyes met Becky's. "To keep him with me." She added. Becky nodded, knowingly. She had been through the social services rigmarole herself, didn't need it explained to her.

"Not everyone understands the sacrifices we have to make for your children. " She told Cindy reassuringly, urging her to continue. Cindy relaxed and sat back on her haunches. She took a gulp of wine.
Becky waited.

"So… I started working as an Escort…"

Becky's reaction was mild surprise. She nodded. "Ok. So, like…"

"Just going on dates with rich guys. They pay really well."

"And… you have sex with them?"

Cindy swallowed. "Well this is the thing…" She slowly explained to Becky how she met Jim. The "jobs" he gave her. The parties. How Escorting was supposed to be mainly dates, no sex but if they wanted it they paid more. Becky listened, without a trace of horror or disgust on her face, which had been what Cindy had expected. Instead, she had a sympathetic look on her face all the way through. When Cindy finished, there was a short silence as she let all the information settle. Then Becky spoke.

"Well sounds to me he's been using you all this time." She swigged her wine and poured more in their glasses. Cindy nodded thoughtfully.

"You know, I'm realising that myself now…" she welled up "am I that stupid? To take me this long to see it?" Becky put her glass down quickly and hugged her friend.

"Hey, no! No! Don't say that. You've done nothing wrong."

"It's not something I want to keep doing, Becky..." Cindy sniffed. She broke off the embrace and wiped her nose. "But... but Patrick... I know he's just a client but he seems different from the other ones." She looked up. "He said he likes me."

Becky shrugged. "They all say that. But if you're stuck doing this, you might as well do it with someone you like back."

"I didn't tell you I liked him back..."

"Oh come on, it's written all over your face! Every time you say his name!"

They laughed. Cindy felt better. "Well, I think I have a plan anyway." She told Becky about her idea to keep the high paying job and save up in secret. How she would leave Jim and make a life for herself.

"See?" Becky smiled proudly at her. "You're smart. That is exactly what you should do. Get away from that arse." They clinked their glasses. "And anything you need, I'm here, ok?"

Cindy felt a huge weight fall from her shoulders. For the first time she had someone she could rely on. For real this time. She put her glass down and gave Becky a hug.

"God I love you girl…" she said gratefully and squeezed her tight. Becky laughed.

"What are besties for eh?"

***

"Have a nice time?" Jim smirked when Cindy walked in with Callum trailing behind. She sensed he wasn't in a better mood and rolled her eyes when she turned around to take her coat off.

"Yeah, it was really nice. Boys had fun, didn't you Callum?" Callum kicked off his shoes and nodded.

"Can I watch TV?" he asked. Jim strode over from where he stood in the kitchen doorway and ruffled the boy's hair.

“Sure you can sport.” Callum hurried to the living room and in a second the noise from some frantic cartoon emanated from the room.

“Turn it down a bit” Cindy called but Jim interrupted her.

“It’s ok bud, it’s fine.” He turned to Cindy, almost menacingly. “Let him watch his cartoons.”

She swallowed and nodded. He was definitely in one of his moods.

“I have to take a shower.” She said and pushed past him but his meaty hand grabbed her wrist, holding a little too tight. Cindy glanced at the living room door. Thankfully they were out of Callum’s sight. Jim leaned into her ear and whispered.

“Get cleaned up nice, I’ve got a job for you.” He let go of her hand. Cindy turned to him with surprise.

“Today? Jim, I’m tired…”

“Not my problem if you stayed up late. Get ready. Milly is coming in an hour to watch Callum.” He let go of her. Cindy rubbed her wrist.

“Who is it?” Had he already spoken to Patrick?

Jim crossed his arms and raised an eyebrow.

"That for me to know and you to find out."

"Jim…"

"You were hoping it's your new lover boy?"

Great. He was not only in a mood, he was in one of his jealous ones. And this time he wasn't far off the truth either… Cindy put on her most incredulous voice.

"What the fuck are you talking about?"

"Patrick Harrison? Mr Exclusive? Yeah, I've been doing some thinking and I'm thinking I don't like what I'm hearing."

Cindy rolled her eyes with a huff. "Really babe? You think I gave the idea or something?"

"Did you?"

Cindy swallowed. "Of course not." She quickly added. "He's just a job."

"Then stop asking about him and let me run this business how I see fit, ok?"

This business. That was all she was to him. Cindy breathed and reminded herself to play her part. She forced a smile.

"Alright babe, calm down. I'll go get ready." She slinked away before he had a chance to say anything else.

She got showered and changed, all the time wondering what he had arranged. It was Sunday afternoon, not the usual time rave parties went on for. She oiled and plaited her hair and put on a low cut black dress without a bra. She had done this a thousand times, like it or not she was a professional of sorts.

When she stepped out of the bedroom, Milly was sitting with Callum in the living room. She waved at them.

"Mummy is going out with Jim, be good for Milly now ok?" Callum nodded and she walked down the corridor to Jim who was now in clean jeans and a jacket. Not like him to smarten up, Cindy wondered. "Where are we going?" She finally asked when they got in his car. It had been a long, silent descent in the elevator. Jim started the engine and drove off.

"The Hilton" was all he said.

So, it was another posh job. Cindy wondered how much this was making him. Was it more than what Patrick offered? She felt nerves rise inside.

The drive was just as silent as the elevator. Jim threw the car around corners and honked impatiently at the traffic. Cindy tried to elicit some answers from him but all she'd had was grunts and a snappy *just do as you're told*. When they finally pulled up outside the Hilton, Jim handed her a piece of paper with a number on it.

"Room 217. Don't go to reception, go straight up, they're expecting you."

"They?"

"Just two guys. Is that a problem?" he glared at her. She swallowed and shook her head. "Good. You've done more than two in a night, you can handle them" he spat. Cindy felt the words hit her like a slap. So, he was punishing her then. For daring to favour one client. As if reading her thoughts, Jim leaned in with a knowing smirk. “And they’re paying what *he* was offering, *each*.” He leaned back, with a satisfied look on his face. “*That’s* how you do business.”

Cindy was shocked. That would mean that just with one job, they were getting at least ten grand. Her cut would be… She did the maths quickly in her head and her fear dissipated. She would and could do this. She needed that money.

“Ok babe, I’ll make sure I’ll get the money up front.” She reached for the door handle and Jim’s words struck her like a blow.

“No need. It’s already transferred to my account. Just in time too, paid off that shitting debt Mark got us in.”

Cindy turned to him.

“All of it?”

“Yup.”

“So…” she swallowed “what about my share?” she muttered. Jim gave her a look.

"You've got a roof over your head. Don't be an ungrateful bitch."

"No." She quickly backtracked. "Of course."

"Get going. I can't wait here so I'll be in the pub. Call me when you're done."

Cindy nodded and climbed out of the car. Her world was shattering. Was what Jim playing at? He never took direct transfers… If he did, she would never get her cut…

She dragged her feet through the lobby and made her way up to the hotel room he had told her. Trembling with anger and nerves, she knocked on the door. She heard voices on the other side and composed herself.

The door opened and a greying man in his fifties stood there, his eyes taking her in.

"I'm Cindy." She remembered to smile. The man was smartly dressed, in a tailored business suit and was swirling a large whisky on ice in his hand. He grinned like a wolf.

"Come in darling…" He stepped aside for her and she walked past him, feeling his eye caress her butt as she moved. In the corner of the large room was an ornate armchair, where another man sat. He also had a scotch in his hand and was appraising her with his eyes, up and down. He looked younger, forties maybe, with grey around his temples and a similar tailored suit.

"Well well, the guy delivered…" He said and stood up. Behind her, the older guy came close and placed a hand on the curve of her butt cheek.

"Shall we get started?" He muttered and kissed the back of her neck.

Cindy cringed inside but smiled sweetly as the second man approached and pressed his mouth on hers.

Within minutes, her dress was in heap on the floor and she was on all fours on the bed, sucking the older man's penis. He lay moaning with pleasure as he guided her head up and down, holding a fistful of her hair. Cindy's mind was already blank, he lips working on him like she was nothing but a machine. She felt the second guy take hold of her hips and the bed jiggled as he knelt on it behind her.

She felt his erection slide into her and closed her eyes. The pounding began. She made herself feel nothing, be nothing. Just a body, with no feeling or emotions. The men's moans washed over her and she let their hands do the work, moving her where they wanted her, like a lifeless doll.

***

Chapter 11

The wind had picked up a chill by that evening and Cindy shivered outside the Hilton lobby. In their haste, she hadn't thought to bring a coat and she was now regretting the low cut dress. She scanned the road for Jim's car, ignoring the knowing look that the doorman was giving her. He knew exactly why she was there, she was sure. Like she was also sure she wasn't the first girl to stand out here shivering in a tiny dress…

Jim's car swayed around the corner and arrived with a screech in front of her. Finally. She yanked the door open and jumped in. He'd had the heating running and she shoved her hands on the air vents, rubbing them to warm up.

"All good?" Jim smiled. He seemed a bit more relaxed and Cindy could smell the beer on his breath. He'd had a couple then.

"Yup, all good." She rubbed her warmed hands on her thighs. Jim drove off, giving the doorman a glare, then laughing. He put his hand on Cindy's thigh. "Hey babe, look, I'm sorry I got snappy with you earlier."

"It's ok."

"You know how I get when I'm stressed."

"Yeah." His hands stroked her thigh.

"They want any funny business?" Cindy shook her head no. "Good. Cos that shit's extra. If they ever do, you tell 'em." He squeezed her thigh and put his hand back on the gearshift. Cindy wrapped her arms around her and curled into a ball, trying to stay warm. Jim reached awkwardly in the back seat, the car swaying a bit.

"Jim, watch out!" He had a habit of driving after a couple of drinks. He was a big guy and could handle it, he said. Cindy was never convinced but the alternative, walking or taking a bus home in this cold was not an option.

"It's alright babe, I'm good." He straightened the car and dragged his jacket from the back seat. "Here, you look frozen." He handed it to Cindy and she wrapped it around her.

"Thanks." She muttered and stayed huddled in her seat, quiet for the rest of the journey. She was exhausted from the hotel and from her late night with

Becky. The warm air from the heating vents filled the car and slowly lulled her to a doze.

She dreamt of Patrick. He was standing on the balcony of a penthouse, but not in London. The view was of a white sandy beach, with palm trees in clumps along the shore. He turned around and his eyes were the same colour of the water behind him.

"Cindy" he whispered and put out his hand. She reached and took it and he pulled her close, gently, like she was gliding on air. His perfect blue eyes looked won into hers and his lips came close, their warmth brushing her own. His fingers caressed a line down her back, all the way to her hip and further.

"Wakey wakey." Jim's voice cut through and she opened her eyes with a startle. He chuckled at her confusion. "What were you smiling at, fast asleep?" he said and leaned across to bring his face close to hers. His massive frame took up nearly all the space she had and his lips crushed hers. She could taste the stale remnants of his beers on him. She pushed him off gently.

"Jim, I need a shower. I'm knackered."

"Mmm, baby, you know I get horny for you after a drink." He leaned in to kiss her again Cindy found the door latch and opened it.

"Not now. Come on." She got out, leaving him pouting like a little boy in the car.

"Ok, ok" he complied. They got out of the car and into the building. In the elevator, Jim kept his hands on her, stroking her buttocks. Cindy let him. She knew what he wanted and she knew he wasn't drunk enough to forget about it.

Milly had already put Callum to bed and he was fast asleep when they walked in. Jim paid her in cash and Cindy thanked her as she let herself out. The door shut and Cindy sighed. Better get it over with.

"I'm going for a shower" she said and went to the bathroom. She left the door unlocked and took off her dress and knickers. The water ran hot and steam quickly filled the small cubicle. She stepped in and sighed with relief under the hot jet, closing her eyes.

She let the water through her hair, down her back then her front, turning this way and that. She didn't hear the door open and close until Jim slid the latch to lock it.

She opened her eyes and through the steamed up glass she could make out his dark, hulking figure, standing naked on the other side. The glass partition slid open and there he was, a leery grin on his face and his enormous black cock standing to attention. He stepped in and slid the glass shut behind him, his cock slapping against her thigh as he turned.

“I hope you saved something for me...” he whispered in her ear as his hands slid along her wet skin, up and down her waist. “I’m getting a bit jealous...” he pouted again and kissed her. His lips were hard, crushing her, sucking her mouth into his. Cindy winced and tried to pull away.

“Jim, you’re hurting me!” she managed when he pulled away.

“Oh sorry babe... don’t know my own strength...” he chuckled, moving closer so the water cascaded on both of them. He took her hand and placed it on his cock. “I just want some of your sugar... I’ll be gentle, sorry...” He pushed her hand up and down his penis and let her carry on stroking him. He busied himself with her breasts, squeezing and sucking, twisting her nipples. Cindy brought both hands to his cock and felt his hands go to her shoulders and push her down. She knelt carefully in the slippery cubicle and took him in her mouth, sucking softly.

"Aargh, yes!" he moaned with delight "Suck it baby, yes!" he grabbed her hair in both hands and moved his hips back and forth. Cindy's tongue worked circles around the tip, licking and flicking. He groaned. "Fuck yes."

Cindy worked on him for a few minutes, taking him deep into her throat when he pushed. She brought her hands to his balls and squeezed gently, all the time licking his shaft. Jim moaned above her. Then, with her hair still in his hands, he yanked her up and turned her around. Cindy braced herself against the wall as one of his arms wrapped around her waist. Jim pulled her close, squashing his penis on her back, grinding on her as his other hand came round and grabbed her vagina. Cindy let out a small squeal of surprise. His giant hand cupped her completely.

"Does that feel good?" Jim slurred and rubbed hard. Cindy grunted. Jim parted her lips with two fingers and jabbed his middle finger inside her. "Does it?" he insisted. Cindy nodded. "Yeah, all you chicks like a bit of fingering innit?" he reached further and shoved another finger in, all the while grinding his thick penis on her back and buttocks. With his fingers inside her, he grabbed so hard he nearly lifted her off the floor.

"Jim..." Cindy puffed. His fingers jabbed roughly, his mouth sucked the skin on her neck.

"Are you wet for me?" he groaned in her ear. "Got some sugar for Big Jim?"

Cindy nodded and his fingers came away, so did is other hand. He grabbed her hips and positioned his already dripping tip at her plump pussy. Cindy had just enough time to brace herself against the tiles. He pushed greedily, with an almighty groan, flesh sliding effortlessly into flesh. Cindy gasped. His hand slid forward again and he reached for her clitoris. He rubbed her mound clumsily and Cindy felt nothing but the ramming of his cock inside her.

She pushed against the tiles, meeting his thrusts, grinding a bit to make him come faster. Jim's hand left her front and, lost in his own pleasure, came to rest on her butt as he fucked her in his semi-drunken stupor. Cindy could feel him pulling out almost completely and pushing the full length of his cock inside her with every thrust. His breathing became faster, turned to gasping, and suddenly he grabbed both hips and shoved himself forward with an almighty shudder. He jerked as he came, his hands digging hard into her flesh as he pressed her onto him, groaning.

Cindy closed her eyes and sighed. Finally she could get some rest.

***

Monday morning found her still reeling from her weekend. She managed to get up in time to get Callum ready for school, while Jim snored his hangover away in bed. After their shower fuck he'd cracked open another few beers. To celebrate, he'd said, their new venture. Cindy had only a few sips before he was already snoring on the sofa. She had taken herself to bed and only vaguely remembered hearing him stumble to bed at some point in the night.

Their new venture… *His* new venture. The more Cindy let realisation sink in, the angrier and more resentful she became. How had she been so naïve, so stupid as to think she'd had a good thing with Jim? What and idiot.

Callum had chatted all the way to school and she had nodded and responded on autopilot but her mind was on other things. She tried to figure out how to get the information she wanted out of Jim. She had thought she'd had him in the palm of her hand, but he'd bamboozled her. Did he sense that she wanted out? Maybe, and if so, what had she done to give it away?

He had found new clients. Those dirty old creeps with their money were not the sort she had expected. She had envisioned more men like Patrick, with class and manners who knew how to treat a lady. But Jim, he had a way of finding the worse. Well, Cindy was not going to spend her days fucking dirty old men in hotel rooms. She had to get her plan to work, she had to find a way to make Patrick her only client.

But how? Jim had all the contacts. She had no access to his files and now it seemed no access to the money either. Her money. Her own fucking money that she had earned with her own sweat. What had Jim done to deserve it?

Becky waved at her across the playground. Cindy raised a hand but the look on her face must have said it all. Becky hurried over, letting Logan run off to play with Callum before the bell rang.

"Hey, what's up?" she asked with concern. Cindy grimaced.

"He's a twat." She hissed out of earshot of little children.

"Let me guess. Jim?"

"A massive wanker." Cindy crossed her arms in anger. She didn't know who she was more furious with Jim or her own stupid self. "What the hell am I doing
Becky?"

Becky stroked her back. "Hey. Stop blaming yourself." The bell rang and the kids all lined up to go to their classrooms. They waved at their boys and watched them march in. Becky snaked her arm into Cindy's. "Come on. I 'm on the late shift today. Let's get a coffee and talk this shit through."

Cindy sighed and let Becky lead her out of the school to the café on the corner. What would she do without Becky?

Chapter 12

Jim was out of bed by the time Cindy returned. He was lounging with a coffee on the sofa, scrolling his phone. Cindy had hoped he'd gone out so she could have some time to herself.

"That you babe?" he called.

"Yeah." Cindy muttered and went in the kitchenette. She could do the dishes or something and avoid sitting with him.

"Babe, you won't believe it" Jim called and she heard his heavy footsteps along the corridor. She turned on the taps and filled the washing up bowl. He came to the door and waved his phone at her. She kept her back to him as she washed up.

"Those guys yesterday? They have some serious connections! I've barely woken up and had three calls already!"

Cindy's shoulders sagged. No. She was not doing this. "Jim…" she began but he was lost in his excitement.

"I've got back to one of them, they want you tonight at the Hilton again."

"Jim…"

"And if I book the other two this week… babe, we'll be rolling in it!"

"*YOU* will be rolling it in!" Cindy surprised herself with the force of her tone. She saw Jim's eyes widen and a moment's fear crossed her heart. But her anger was stronger. No. Enough. She'd had enough of his shit.

"Babe, what are you talking about?" Jim sweettalked her. "It's like, ten grand a night with these dudes!"

"Yeah and what do you have to do for it, huh? You're not the one spreading your legs and being groped, but you are the one taking all the money, right?"

"Hey, I told you, I had to pay off Mark's debt. You'll get your cut this time."

"My cut is peanuts and you know it."

"Bullshit! Who puts a roof over your head huh?" He was getting angry now.

"Oh don't give me that crap. I'm not doing it."

"What?"

"I'm not doing it. Find another girl."

"Cindy. Don't fuck me about now. I made the booking. They paid half already." He walked menacingly towards her and shoved a finger in her face. She didn't flinch. "You are going to the fucking Hilton tonight and you're gonna do as you're fucking told, you hear me?" They glared at each other for a long, silent moment. Jim smirked. "Yeah, I thought so." He stepped away and turned to leave. "Ungrateful little whore."

"Fuck you." The words came out of Cindy's mouth unbidden. Yeah, fuck him and the assholes who used her like a piece of meat.

"What did you say?" Jim turned slowly, incredulous.

"You fucking heard me. I'm out."

His arm moved with lightning speed. He backhanded her so hard, Cindy lost her balance and fell onto the sink. She tasted blood in her mouth and red droplets stained the dishwater beneath her. Before she had time to react, his hand was on her hair, yanking her head back, close to his face. Spittle flew from his lips as he yelled.

"You fucking disobey me again and you *WILL* be out! Out on the *STREET*. You *and* your little brat! Do you understand me?" Cindy was in shock. He shook her violently by the hair and she winced. "DO YOU?"

She nodded, out of habit and desperation more than anything. Jim shoved her away with disgust. Cindy brought a hand to her bleeding mouth, her eyes stinging with angry tears. Jim threw a tea towel at her.

"Clean yourself up. You got a job tonight." He stormed out. Cindy pressed the towel to her face, shaking. The shock wore off and her fury rose again. She stayed in the kitchen, listening to his angry stomping around the flat, until he slammed the front door and left without another word at her. Cindy knew he'd be out a while, probably down the pub to drink his anger away and make his "business" calls.

Well, if he thought she was going to stay home, trembling like a little mouse, he had another thing coming. Cindy meant what she said. Fuck him.

She rushed to her room and pulled her stash of money from the closet. She had managed to squirrel away a couple of thousand in cash. It was enough for now. She found a suitcase and packed as many of her things as she could, then emptied Callum's drawers. When the suitcase was full, she packed shopping bags. She worked frantically, wanting to get out before Jim got back. When she was satisfied she had everything she needed she called a taxi and hauled her stuff to the lift.

The driver helped her get everything in the car and drove her to the address she gave him. If he'd noticed the cut on her lip, he didn't say anything and Cindy was glad of it. When they arrived, he helped her unload everything again and she paid him in cash, then sat on her suitcase to wait.

It was just past 3pm when Becky walked down the street in her cleaning uniform. She spotted Cindy on her doorstep and frowned. When she saw the bags surrounding her, her face dropped. She hurried over the the house.

"Hey... You ok?" she asked and her eyes landed on the purple bruise on Cindy face. "Oh fuck… babe…" She ran over and gave her a hug. Cindy's composure finally melted and she let her tears flow on her friends' shoulder.

"Hey, it's ok, come on, come inside…"

Becky opened the door and together they carried her stuff into the house. Cindy sniffed and calmed down.

"I didn't know where else to go… I don't want to intrude…"

"Don't be silly. You did the right thing."

"I have some money, I'll find a place. We just need somewhere for now…"

Becky hugged her again. "Hey. You stay here as long as you need, ok? I meant it when I said anything you need. Anything."

Cindy held on tight. "Thank you."

"Not a problem." Becky checked the time. "Look, I have to pick up Logan and drop him off at Malcolm's before my next shift. Do you want me to take Callum too? Malcolm won't mind."

Cindy hadn't even thought about that. She couldn't turn up at school with her face a mess… "Oh gosh, could you?"

"Of course. I'll do that, you make yourself a cuppa, relax, ok?"

"Ok, thank you."

"Does… he know where you are?"

"He doesn't know where you live."

"Ok. Well, look, just call the police if you have to, if he finds the house. Ok?"

"Ok. Thank you Becky."

"Oh, babe, stop it. Come here" she embraced her again and kissed her good cheek. "I'm here for you. Now, get some ice on that. I'll see you after work."

Cindy nodded and Becky got a key out of a drawer on the sideboard. "Here, keep the doors locked when I'm gone." She handed her the key and left. Cindy locked the door behind her and sat on the stairs, looking at all her possessions in her friend's hallway. The silence of the house enveloped her and she sighed.

Finally, she let tears of relief flow. She was free.

***

It took Jim less than three days to find her. He had connections all around town and it had not been hard to find her best friend's address. He had come to the house and even the school gates, but keeping him away had proven just as easy. Cindy hadn't even had to call the police – the threat alone was enough. Jim's dealings meant that the last thing he wanted was the police on his back. And, other than their argument, he had nothing against her. She hadn't stolen from him and they hadn't been married so there was no legal standing for him to pursue. And he knew full well whose side the law would take, especially with proof literally marked on her face.

Of course that hadn't stopped him telling her what he thought of her, but his obscenities no longer bothered Cindy. He couldn't touch her, she had made sure of it by taking photos of her bruised face and making it clear to him that if he ever came near her or Callum again, she would make sure the photos and everything she knew about his "business" were seen by the police. It was all the arsenal she needed.

After two weeks of empty threats from him and real threats from her, he disappeared. Occasionally Cindy would glimpse him in the pub or on the street but he only glared and let her be. As the weeks went by, see saw new girls hanging of his arm or following him like puppies on the street. She felt sorry for them but she had also hardened inside. They had their lives to live and she had her own. Let them find out the hard way just like she had.

Her money lasted longer than she had expected, mainly because Becky refused to take a penny off her for rent. She had moved into her spare room and Callum was delighted to be sharing a room with Logan. Becky had managed to get Cindy a couple of cleaning shifts a week and over time she picked up a few more, adding to her little savings as she went along.

Weeks turned into months and Cindy was conscious of not wanting to abuse her friend's hospitality. They were perfect housemates, but Cindy had made it clear that it was a temporary arrangement. She would find her feet and once she had enough working hours behind her to show for, she would apply to the council for her own place.

She missed nothing of her old life. Her body was finally her own, not some sex toy for random men to abuse for their pleasure. She belonged to no-one but herself, and the knowledge gave her a new sense of power. She took pride in her new job and worked hard, always on time and diligent. She relished her paycheque, small as it was. It wasn't much, but it was all hers. She didn't even miss having sex. Well, the work sex anyway…

More than once her mind had wandered to her time with Patrick and the magical feelings he had raised in her. He had been nothing but a client of course, and only for two dates, but something had definitely sparked between them. It was the only regret she had about leaving, losing him. She knew in her heart that his request for exclusivity was only a first step towards something more. She didn't know how she knew that but she was certain it was not just a girlish fantasy. Men who paid for sex did not treat the girls the way he had. There had been something else there.

She sighed every time she thought of him. He was lost to her now. Jim had all the contacts and in her haste she had not thought to look for his files. All she had was a name: Patrick Harrison. She had of course googled him on Becky's computer and a million Patrick Harrisons had popped up. She looked up a few but it would take her days to find him. And if she did, then what? It had been months since she last saw him. A man like him would have met countless other girls by now, all vying for his looks and attention. And of course, Cindy reminded herself bitterly, they would all be worthy of his calibre. Posh girls from rich families with good educations, connections and class.

There may have been sparks between them those two nights but the fire would have never caught. They were worlds apart.

***

Chapter 13

Life settled into a new sort of normality for Cindy. Becky and she took separate shifts with the cleaning agency, so one would be able to look after the kids. Sometimes they would have Tom over too and sometimes Malcolm had all the kids so the girls could go out or take the same shift. The arrangement worked and Cindy found herself in pleasant company all the time. There were no more raves and the only parties she'd been to, were the various kids' birthdays that Logan and Callum had been invited to.

Slowly and steadily, she was accepted into the circle of school mums. She was sure her story had circulated through the playground grapevine, as their sympathetic looks and pointed *"how are you doing"* questions revealed. Obviously they didn't know the details, but it had only take one glimpse at her slowly healing face and learning that she had left her partner for them to piece their own story together.

It suited her. Her story was just enough of a mystery to elicit kindness from them, without asking too many questions. She often went straight to school to pick up the boys after a shift, without changing out of her cleaning uniform. It gave her pleasure to know that the other parents now looked at a working single mum, not some gold-digging trollop. She hoped the uniform shamed them into realising how wrong they had been about her.

Her diligence at work had also paid off. She was getting more shifts and some of the better paid jobs too; big, detached houses in the suburbs and corporate offices in the City. She had to travel for some of those but the pay was worth it and the company was fair and covered part of her expenses. The council had also put her and Callum on a waiting list for a house so all she had to do was keep working, and wait. Cindy was finally making a life for herself.

She had even saved up enough to keep herself and Callum in comfort. She was sensible with her money and although Becky refused rent, she insisted on at least covering half of the food and bills. She treated Logan at the café just the same as Callum when they went and revelled in how happy her little boy was becoming. She had thought he was happy around Jim, but realised there was always an underlying weariness around him. Callum had become a lot more relaxed and cooperative, and hadn't had a tantrum in months.

Her new friends were more like family. At Tom's birthday, Becky and herself had stayed behind to help Malcolm clear up and spent the rest of the evening relaxing and chatting, just the three of them. They shared a lot in common, especially their love for their children. The six of them made for a strange, but loving little family, and Cindy was grateful to have them. Her life was simple, but happy, and she didn't need anything to change.

***

Cindy pushed the vacuum cleaner through the endless cubicles of the office floor. She had been to this building before and knew all the nooks and crannies that needed cleaning. She hummed to herself under the noise of the machine, working her way around the desks. The kitchen area would be next and emptying all the bins. In about a half hour she would be done and able to get home early. These office jobs may be better paid but they were late in the day, after everyone had left work. It was March and the days were longer but the sun was already dipping in the horizon.

She liked the offices in the City, especially the ones right at the top of the skyscrapers. From here, she could see across the whole of London and she did that now, standing at the large glass windows, watching the grey disk of the sun in the hazy distance. It was a spectacular view whatever the weather and Cindy loved how different it was every time.

She tucked the hoover away in the supplies cupboard and cleaned the kitchen surfaces. With that done, she dried her hands on her apron and changed the black bag in the large bin. The full one she then carried through the offices, emptying the smaller bins into it. She then made her way to the walled-off offices at the far end and the large conference rooms. At the last one, she nearly jumped out of her skin when she opened the door.

"Oh my gosh, I'm so sorry!" she apologised at the suited man that sat behind the large desk. "I thought everyone was gone… I'm sorry." She backed out of the door and the man waved at her with a smile.

"It's ok darling, please do what you need. Just a late meeting, sorry we startled you."

Cindy nodded, slightly embarrassed to have interrupted and stepped back into the room, vaguely aware of a second person she hadn't notice the first time. She scuttled to the bin and smiling politely, emptied the contents into the black bag. Just as quickly, she hurried out again, pausing briefly on her way out.

"I'm so sorry to bother - " she muttered and the words caught in her throat as she glimpsed the second man's face.

Patrick.

A look of astonishment passed between them for the briefest of moments. Cindy panicked, blurted another apology and shut the door quickly. Her heart raced along with her feet and she ran the distance between the office and the exit. She pushed through the heavy fire doors and pressed the lift button frantically.

"Come on… Come on…" The illuminated number at the top showed 7. She was on the 34th floor…

To her left, another door led to the stairs. Cindy looked from the lift panel to the stair doors, weighing her options. Her feet were killing her from working all afternoon. The lift was now at the 8th floor. Her heart was beating like drum in her ears. Adrenaline urged her on. She turned for the stairs.

"Cindy?"

His voice sent an electric current through her body. She froze. Realised she still held the full bin bag in her hand and grimaced. This was a nightmare.

"I thought it was you." Patrick's voice was closer now. Still sending her quivering inside after all those months. She gripped the bag tighter, gritted her teeth. The last time he saw her she looked like a princess. Now she was a drab mess, with a stinking bag of rubbish in her hand.

"Are you not going to say anything?" his voice was soft, but insistent. Cindy sighed. Too late to run now. She turned to face him and the same blue eyes bore into her, just like she remembered.

"Hi Patrick..." she mumbled. If only the earth could swallow her now. He was looking at her with an odd mixture of amusement and surprise. And… was there something else? He stepped closer.

“I never heard from you again. Or… well… your… you know…”

“I’m sorry. I don’t do that… work anymore.”

“Oh.” There was more approval in that sound than surprise. He reached for her hand and Cindy flinched.

“Please…” she shook her head “don’t.”

“Why?” Patrick ignored her and took her hand in his anyway. He stroked it gently as he spoke. “Are you embarrassed? About… what we did?”

It was Cindy’s turn to be surprised. Here she was looking like Cinderella and he thought she was ashamed of *him*? She couldn’t help but laugh.

“I was never embarrassed about what we did.” She smiled at the memory. “But I’m not that girl anymore. Look at me. Not exactly… presentable.”

Patrick moved closer and there was mirth in his eyes. “Well, if I remember well, it wasn’t the presentation I was interested in.” He was standing so close now Cindy could feel his body heat. She shook her head sadly.

"Patrick... Don't toy with me, please..."

"Who said I'm toying with you?" He leaned in and his face was close to hers, his breath warm on her skin. She inhaled the memory of his skin on hers. "When I said I liked you, I meant it." he whispered and touched her lips lightly with his. Cindy's heart fluttered like a bird in a too-small cage. She dropped the bag. Patrick pulled back and smiled down at her, with a twinkle in his eye.

"I thought I'd never see you again." He said and Cindy threw her arms around his neck. Their kiss was long and passionate, making up for months of missed chances.

***

The bus ride back was a blur and walking back from the bus stop felt like walking on air. Cindy was completely and utterly railroaded and couldn't wait to tell Becky what had happened. Her smile stretched from ear to ear and her heart had not stopped beating like mad all the way.

The boys were eating their dinner when she walked in, and Becky was making tea. She took one look at Cindy and her eyes widened.

"What happened to you?" She said. "You're grinning like the Cheshire cat!"

"You won't believe who I met at work…"

Becky's hands flew to her mouth. "Noooo…!" Cindy nodded, unable to stop grinning. "Oh my God, you have to tell me all about it!" She picked up the tea and handed Cindy one. She told the boys to eat up and call her for pudding and ushered Cindy into the living room.

"So? Spill the beans!" She shook with excitement. Cindy recounted how she had bumped into Patrick, how she had nearly missed him actually, hadn't even seen him standing there. If he hadn't seen her too, she might have walked right past him. She told her how she'd panicked sending Becky into hoots of laughter and then how he had chased after her. Becky sighed, riveted. And Cindy told her about their kiss, how they couldn't let go of each other. But he'd had to get back to his meeting, so they exchanged numbers and he took her address.

"This address?" Becky asked. Before Cindy had a chance to reply, there was a knock on the door. They looked at each other with surprise.

"What…?" Becky muttered. "Weird…!" She went to the door and a moment later called out "It's for you!"

Cindy frowned and followed her. A delivery guy stood on the porch, with a huge bouquet of red roses awkwardly held in front of him.

"Miss Cindy Vickers?" his muffled voice came from his helmet.

"Yes, that's me" Cindy walked over incredulous, while Becky stood to one side, finding the situation very amusing. She took the flowers for the man.

"It's heavy" he warned her and it was. She realised the flowers were in a vase of some sort. She had to put it on the floor when she realised the man was handing her a second item, a small gift-wrapped parcel. She took that too and, confused, signed the pad he held out for her. He nodded and left.

"What the hell?" Cindy muttered and closed the door. Becky picked up the flowers and set them on the sideboard. Cindy pulled the wrapping off and revealed a beautifully cut crystal vase.

"Wow…" Becky exclaimed. She reached in the bouquet and plucked the small embossed card that was nested in the stems.

"What does it say?" Cindy asked.

"Exclusively yours, Patrick." Becky read out loud. "Oh my God Cindy, how romantic."

Cindy had no words. Her insides were turning to jelly. She had forgotten all about the parcel in her hands.

"What's that then?" Becky reminded her and her shocked gaze finally moved from the stunning flowers to her hands. She tore the paper and let it fall to the floor. Wrapped inside, was a leather bound flat box with a gold clasp. She looked at Becky. Becky looked at her.

They swallowed.

Cindy undid the clasp and opened the box. Inside, perfectly nestled in the softest black velvet, was gleaming pearl necklace. It lay in a semi-circle in the box, in the middle of which was a matching bracelet, flanked by two pearl earrings with tiny tear-drop shaped diamonds hanging from their bases. Cindy was speechless.

"Holy shit" said Becky.

***

Chapter 14

"There's a limo! There's a limo!" Callum and Logan shouted up from the front room where they had been stood at the window like sentinels.

"Shit, I'm not ready…" Cindy fumbled with her earrings. The boys hooted from downstairs and Becky had to shout from the landing for them to pipe down.

"Let me help you." She said to a nervous Cindy when she went back to the room. She was stood in front of the full-length mirror, checking everything from her dress to her make-up and hair.

"Girl, calm. Let him wait a little." Becky smiled and helped her clasp the pearls around her neck. They stood admiring them in the mirror. "They look stunning on you hun…" Becky said. Cindy had to agree. The creamy white beads shone like little moons against her dark skin. The earrings were the same, the dangling diamonds sparkling as they caught the light.

She smoothed her dress – the same red dress she had worn on their first date. It was the obvious choice when she had gone through her wardrobe. Since leaving Jim, she hadn't needed anything fancy but she had held on to her beautiful dresses all the same. Maybe it was them that had brought her good luck.

"Ok, how do I look?"

"You look amazing, stop fretting!"

"Ok."

"Now go. Prince Charming awaits!" she gave an excited jiggle and followed Cindy down the stairs. Callum and Logan had their faces pressed at the window, gaping at the black limo out front.

"Callum, be good now, ok?" Cindy kissed him and hugged Logan and went out the door with an excited wave from Becky. She saw the car and felt a rush of excitement. It was a limo, the boys had been right. Not just a car like the other times she had been picked up.

She took a step down the garden path and the back door opened. Patrick stepped out, looking like Prince Charming indeed. He was in a silk black tuxedo that almost simmered in the street light as he came around to her side. He smiled with pure joy at seeing her and gallantly held the door open for her. Cindy took a deep breath and couldn't hide the joy on her own face at seeing him. She walked down the rest of the path to meet him.

"You look beautiful." Patrick said and pecked her on the cheek. "I have to behave myself in front of your audience..." he chuckled and Cindy turned to see three faces pressed at Becky's front window, giving her the thumbs up. Cindy groaned and rolled her eyes.

"Oh, I'll kill them later." She laughed and waved at them, then climbed into the limo. Patrick shut the door and came back around to the other side and slid in beside her. Cindy took in their surroundings. It wasn't a stretch limo like she'd seen in the movies but it was big, with plush seats and a mini bar. The driver sat unseen behind a soundproof glass at the front end. Low lighting with soft music turned the back into a romantic hideaway, just for the tow of them.

"This is amazing..." Cindy wondered aloud. Patrick tapped a button on the wall beside him and the car moved off in a smooth motion. He poured two glasses of champagne for them.

"To good fortune and Lady Luck" he toasted and they sipped. "Thank you for accepting my invitation" he added.

"Of course." Cindy replied. "Thank you for inviting me."

"These charity events can get tiresome after a while. They're all the same." Patrick mused. "It's much better if one has good company along."

Cindy blushed. She drank her champagne and Patrick topped her up.

"So, where are we going?" she asked.

"West End somewhere. I don't even bother looking at the addresses anymore, James knows where to take us." He waved a hand in the direction of the driver. "I just get told where to turn up, I smile, spend a good bit of money and everyone's happy." He sighed. "Just part of the job."

Cindy nodded, as if she knew exactly what he was talking about. Well, maybe she did in a way. Her job had also been to go where she was told, smile and look pretty. Only she had to spend other people's money. But not anymore, she reminded herself. Patrick had *invited* her. Not *booked* her. She was for real his legitimate date for the night.

"Well, hopefully I'll help you have more fun tonight" she said and let the hidden meaning of her words drift between them. Patrick smiled and kissed her.

"Oh I'm sure you will" he whispered, kissing her again. Their lips met again and again and Cindy felt a sudden surge of pent-up passion. God, she wanted him… after all those months of celibacy, she felt herself go wet. She moaned softly and a gentle throbbing began in her vagina. She sensed Patrick's difficulty in pulling away from her too. They drank each other in with their eyes, wanting more but knowing they had to wait.

"Later..." Patrick sighed lustfully. He took a large gulp of champagne and topped up their glasses again. They had a social event to get through first. Cindy took some deep breaths and giggled. Patrick joined her and soon the y were both in fits of giggles. She tried to distract herself from his hot presence with small talk.

"I've never been in a limo before."

"This? Oh this is more like an executive car."

"Oh."

"I keep the limo for the country. It's no use on London roads"

"*Oh*." Cindy was impressed. Two limos? Patrick noticed the awe in her eyes and chuckled.

"Ok, you got me, I'm a bit spoilt." His eyes twinkled. He leaned in conspiratorially and whispered "if you're really good, I might show you the helicopter too. And the yacht..." He winked and Cindy spluttered her champagne.

"Stop it! You're pulling my leg."

Patrick shrugged and grinned. Cindy laughed out loud. The champagne was having an effect and she was loosening up. And this guy, this gorgeous blue eyed guy with his boyish charms was sweeping her off her feet.

"Where did I find you, huh?" She said.

"I think maybe we found each other." Patrick beamed at her.

***

The charity Ball was in yet another high class hotel Cindy hadn't even heard of. She marvelled at how these enormous spaces existed, hidden in the heart of London. Somewhere in the maze of narrow streets and endless traffic, they felt like stepping into another dimension. The lobby was vast and gilded and the huge ballroom was lined with floor to ceiling mirrors that gave the illusion of an infinite space. Chandeliers sparkled above them and sharply dressed waiters glided effortlessly amongst the guest with an endless supply of canapes and drinks.

Like the first time, Cindy watched and learned from the ladies around her. Patrick introduced her to a few people and she watched him charm everyone in his wake. Everyone seemed to know him and they greeted her with genuine pleasure. She drank daintily, not wanting to embarrass herself or Patrick by getting tipsy and danced with him until the music stopped. By the end of the night, she really felt like a Princess on the arm of her Prince.

Back in the limo, Patrick dimmed the lights more and raised the music. He intercommed to the driver to head off and relaxed back in the leather seat. Cindy did the same, leaning close to him. She rested her head on his shoulder and took his hand.

"Thank you" she said "I had a wonderful time. Patrick brought her hand to his mouth and kissed it.

"My pleasure." He kissed the tip of each of her fingers and his blue eyes bore into hers. "Now, I have a bit of a confession to make…" "Oh yeah?" Cindy asked.

"I was kinda hoping you might like to stay the night."

Cindy smiled and raised her lips to his. She kissed him. "I thought you'd never ask…" she purred. Patrick smiled and nibbled her bottom lip.

"I mean at my place. It's a bit of a long drive though."

"Well, I'm sure we'll find something to do…" Cindy's hand slid up his thigh. Patrick kissed her mouth again and reached for the intercom button.

"James?" he called.

"Sir." Came the tinny voice from the speaker. Cindy's hand moved further up and squeezed his bulge gently. Patrick gasped.

"Erm… Change of plans…" he took a breath as Cindy's fingers found his buttons and began undoing them. "We're going back to mine. Pentonville House."

"Yes sir." Cindy's hand was now sliding inside his silk boxers.

"And James?" Patrick managed. "Take the… scenic route."

"Yes sir."

Cindy felt the car swerve gently as it changed lanes and the music turned up a bit louder. Her hand had found Patrick's cock and she wrapped her fingers around it, feeling him getting hard already.

"Oh, you naughty thing…" Patrick half-gasped, half chuckled. "Naughty naughty thing…"

Cindy turned her body so she could face him. She kissed him again, while her hand freed his erection and stroked him.

"Can James see back here?" she whispered in his ear.

"Do you want him to?" he whispered back. Cindy laughed and slid off the leather seat to the carpeted floor. She licked the tip of his penis and he gasped, his eyes never leaving hers. Cindy wanted to give him all the pleasure she could. And she wanted every bit of him. Her mouth covered his shaft and she sucked him slowly, gently, caressing his full length with her tongue. Patrick lay back moaning with pleasure. He stroked her hair, her neck, her face as she moved her head rhythmically up and down.

"Come here" he whispered between gasps "come to me…" he said and pulled her gently back up to the seat. Cindy kept one hand on his cock, keeping the rhythm going and he slid a hand up her dress, finding her moist and ready. "Oh yes…" he whispered and his mouth closed on hers, their hands working on each other in unison. It was Cindy's turn to moan. "You like that?" His fingers slid inside her while his thumb pressed on her clit, sending currents racing through her. She tugged at his cock more urgently.

"I want you…" her voice came out hoarse "I want you so bad…"

"Now?" he whispered, his fingers working faster on her.

"Yes…" Cindy gasped "yes, please… now… now…"

In a swift move, Patrick was above her. He tore her knickers and threw them in two pieces on the floor. Cindy raised her hips, ready, willing him to enter her. His tip found her wet pussy and when he slid inside her, she thought she would lose her mind. She had wanted this for so long… She pushed her hips further up and he pushed harder, his hand on her firm buttocks, pulling her to him.

Their hunger for each other brought them quickly to a simultaneous climax. Patrick bucked and shoved his cock as far as he could inside Cindy's throbbing pussy, both lost in a silent scream of delight. They held each other for what felt like an aeon, shuddering together, feeling each other pulsate in the throes of their orgasms. Slowly, the waves subsided and the settled in each other's arms, breathless.
Patrick kissed her deeply, his tongue seeking hers.

"The night is still young" he whispered in her ear.

***

Chapter 15

Pentonville House was a ten bedroom mansion in Richmond, with a driveway the size of the school playground and a marble fountain dominating the centre. Hedges as high as Becky's house surrounded the property and a heavy wrought iron gate finished off the perimeter. Inside, the hallway was wide and lavish and a large staircase led up to the top floor. Cindy had seen little else of the inside as they had gone straight to the master bedroom where Patrick took her again, passionately, reaching new heights of pleasure.

Their lovemaking had lasted for hours, each exploring the other with insatiable hunger, until they lay exhausted in each other's arms. In the morning, Patrick had left early for a meeting while Cindy was still asleep. A note waited for her next to another impressive bunch of flowers and a housemaid had served her breakfast and called her *"Ma'am".*

Cindy kept twirling the note in her hand as she sat in the back of the cab that took her home. The flowers were propped on the seat next to her. She read it over and over again. *I can't bear a moment away... Still hungry for you. See me tonight?* She sighed. This was a whole new feeling she was experiencing. She had thought she'd felt it before but this was different.

Was she falling in love?

***

The days went by in a rosy haze for Cindy and spring slowly turned to summer. She saw Patrick almost every day, sometimes meeting him for long lunches at his London offices, or staying over in Richmond. Their passionate sojourns were beyond belief but there was more than sex to their affair. On weekends he took her and Callum on trips to the country and stole Callum's heart with a helicopter ride to the Scilly Isles. When the weather improved, he took them out on his yacht, inviting Becky and Logan too.

He slowly became a fixture of her life and they spent hours talking, nestled in each other's arms in bed or walking hand in hand along the Thames. Gifts continued to arrive at Becky's house, flowers and jewellery, toys for Callum and Logan. Even Becky would get boxes of cakes or rare potted plants to go in her garden. His charm and generosity had no end.

Cindy carried on working, but she let Becky take the better paid shifts at the offices and big houses. She didn't want to lose her sense of independence, but now that she was dating Patrick, it wouldn't do to be seen scrubbing toilets by the same people who saw her dressed up at galas hanging off his arm. Besides, she liked working, it gave her real satisfaction to earn an honest living. She had even started looking at various courses she could take. Nursing perhaps or childminding. She was young and had her whole life ahead of her, she could still make something of herself.

Patrick admired her tenacity. Having heard her story, so different to his own upbringing, he marvelled at the strength she had shown through the hardships and he told her so. He may have been sent to the best schools, he had said, but she had learnt a lot more than him in a lot less time. She was his wise muse, he called her. Cindy always blushed and told him to stop flattering her but he would grow serious and remind her that she had hidden strengths that no other person he knew had. He knew billionaires who held half the world in their hands, but would be reduced to dust if they had faced the challenges she had. *Remember who you are*, he'd say. *You are a rock*.

On Cindy's 22nd birthday, he took all four of them to the theatre and then for a special dinner at the restaurant they had gone for their first dinner date. They'd had a private booth at the furthest end of the restaurant, with the best wine, and every dessert the boys wanted. After dinner, Becky took the boys home, leaving them to enjoy the rest of the evening alone. Cindy hugged each one goodbye, Patrick high-fived Callum and Logan and Becky winked at her when his back was turned.

Back at their table, Patrick slid across the leather seat and slipped his arm around her waist. The waiters cleaned up the party debris around them.

"I have something for you." He said and pulled a small organza gift-bag out of his pocket. "Happy Birthday"

"Oh, Patrick…" Cindy took the little silver bag.

"You've already done so much." He shrugged.

"It's nothing. Open it."

Cindy untied the silk ribbon and pulled the little pouch open. Something metallic glimmered inside. She frowned. "What is it?" She upended the bag and into her open palm fell a house key. She looked at Patrick with confusion. "What…"

"I want you to move in with me."

Cindy was speechless. She looked from him to the key and back again, her mouth opening and closing like a fish. *Move in?*

"I… what…?" was all she could manage. Patrick laughed and cupped her face tenderly in his hands.

"Cindy. You have made my grey, joyless life a dream." His fingers stroked her cheeks softly "I want you with me, near me, all the time. I never realised how empty that house was until you came…" He held her gaze with his blue eyes for a long moment, then kissed her. Cindy's mind reeled.

"Patrick..." she whispered. "Are you sure?" "Never been sure of anything in my life." His hands slid down to find hers and their fingers interlocked. He brought her hand up to his mouth and kissed it. "I love you Cindy. Come live with me."

Cindy threw her arms around him and hugged him so he wouldn't see the tears forming in her eyes. She couldn't believe what she was hearing.

"I love you too." She told him. "I think I've loved you from the first time I saw you." She didn't care how corny that sounded. She realised now that it was true. From the moment she had first set eyes on his handsome face, standing outside the Dorchester that cold November night... It seemed a lifetime ago. She sat back and wiped a tear from her eye. To her surprise, his eyes were also wet. They laughed and kissed, oblivious to the staff still discreetly tidying around them.

"I have another surprise for you..." Patrick whispered and kissed the tip of her nose.

"You're full of those, aren't you?" Cindy said. "What is it?"

"You'll see. Come on."

They got their coats, Patrick paid the bill and holding her by the hand they jumped in his limo that was waiting outside. As soon as the car moved off, his hands were on her, roaming her curves, his mouth on hers. Cindy's body responded. She kissed him back, feeling the tell-tale low throb in her pelvis. She tasted the wine on his warm tongue and his hand moved to the wet spot between her legs.

"Oh, Patrick…" she whispered as he gently stroked her mound. He bit her lower lip and tugged it gently.

"This is just a warm up…" he whispered and moved his fingers as softly as possible, barely tickling her. Cindy gasped, aching for more. He watched her expression, applying gentle pressure now and taking it away. Cindy moved her hips closer and he pulled his fingers away, kissing her ear and whispering seductively to her.

"Not yet gorgeous…"

"Please…" she begged more than once but for the rest of the short journey he had teased her clit, bringing her to the promise of pleasure and taking it away. By the time they reached their destination, Cindy wanted him inside her with ravenous desperation.

She barely recognised the hotel where they'd had their first even night of passion. She tottered with him to the elevator, trying to look composed but heaving with anticipation. When the doors slid shut, she pressed her body on his before the cubicle even began to ascend. She could feel him hard and ready against her, but he kept his cool.

"Not yet gorgeous…" He said again and kissed her deep and long. When her hands frantically tried to claw at his trousers, he took her wrists and lifting her arms, he pinned her against the wall. "I said not yet…" he continued to tease, leaving her panting. She sighed as his eyes bore tantalisingly into hers. Holding her in that way, he pressed against her and kissed her again. Feeling his soft mouth on hers and his hard groin pushing against her willing body, Cindy felt giddy with desire.

"I want you…" she panted "please, take me… take me now…" she begged. Patrick only smirked with that old twinkle in his eye.

The elevator mercifully pinged. The Penthouse. The doors opened and Patrick stepped out backwards, leading her by the hands, just like the first time. It all came flooding back to Cindy as she stumbled after him, desperate for his skin on hers, his cock inside her. His eyes were like a magnet, drawing her into oblivion and she did not even realise how and when their clothes came off and his toned white body was pressed on her ebony skin, his teeth gently nibbling her neck, her back falling on the silken sheets.

"Patrick... Patrick..." she mumbled as his mouth moved with fluttering kisses all along her body, from her neck to her breasts, stopping at each nipple. He teased them each in turn with his tongue and fingers, sucked on them gently, and moved on, further south. Cindy buckled under him, her fingers weaving in his hair, her nails drawing sharp lines on his back. "Oh god... please..." she kept begging and his head came up briefly to look at her with that twinkle again.

"What do you want...?" he asked languidly, and searched her bellybutton with his tongue suggestively. Cindy buckled again and pushed his head down.

"You... I want you... please..."

"Where do you want me?" he went on licking below her bellybutton, moving closer to her quivering mound.

"Inside me… I want you inside me…"

His tongue landed on her clit and she almost howled as the sharp current shot through her. "Yes! Yes!" she shouted, undulating her hips as he sucked on her vulva hungrily. Cindy writhed with pleasure and let out a long, drawn out moan when he slid two fingers in her, stroking her vagina as his tongue pressed hot and hard on her clit.

"Now… Now…!" her breathless voice urged and he came up, positioning himself above her. Cindy raised her knees, opening herself up for him. Her hands slid to his waist and his mouth met hers as he lowered himself and pushed deep and firm inside her.

"Oh God!" she moaned "Oh yes! Yes!" Her nails dug into his skin and she pulled him closer, deeper, her own hips coming up to meet him, his hands on her buttocks, holding her tight against him. His cock was hard as stone and her wet, ready pussy was tight around it, making him grunt with pleasure. Cindy wrapped her legs around him and they moved in perfect unison, lost in a private dance, their pleasure heightening with every thrust.

Cindy heard his breath come in faster gasps and her own body began to reach the peak of its climax. Her moans mingled with his and Patrick shoved his cock hard and deep with one last thrust that sent Cindy into convulsions of delight. They came in unison, gasping for air, shuddering in the throes of their orgasms and Cindy lost herself in a blinding light of pure, animal pleasure.

To Be Continued…

www.ingramcontent.com/pod-product-compliance
Lightning Source LLC
LaVergne TN
LVHW012054160826
845678LV00014B/2828

* 9 7 8 1 7 3 9 5 8 4 1 0 8 *